This book is dedicated to

Choong Chee Chim
1962-1989

Art Director, Ogilvy & Mather Direct, KL
You are much missed, my friend

Table of Contents

Introduction

M_y first memories of Kuala Lumpur are connected to my first car drive to work in that city.

I was staying at a service residence we came to call the Pink Palace.

It was a complex of apartments, arranged in a square, on two levels. In the middle, there was a pool. On one side, two tennis courts.

This was a modest apartment. Two bedrooms, a bath and a sparse kitchen. On the second level. In the heart of KL. Just a few blocks from what is known as the Golden Triangle, an area of the city that was, and still is, a centre of bustle and commerce.

My first travels to the office were by taxi. Then I was given a car.

Car in hand, I had to travel to the suburban city of Petaling Jaya. Is it north, south, east or west of KL? Don't ask. Even now, I don't know. But I do know that on a good day, it's about a 20-minute drive from Kuala Lumpur.

When I first arrived in KL in 1989, cars were not a problem. The problem was motorbikes. Stop your car at an intersection, and motorbike riders became your second, third, fourth and fifth skin. There were hundreds of them.

I remember someone's advice. Don't worry about them. They will take care of themselves. And yet, you do worry. If I accelerate, will I not hit someone? If I shift lanes, will I not knock someone down? If I cut them, will they not bleed?

On top of all that, I was driving on the wrong side of the road. Malaysia follows the English way. I'd been given exemplary directions to the office. Look for this sign, look for that sign. Exit there. And above all, stay on the left side of the highway. Ok.

But I digress. Or perhaps, get ahead of myself.

Let me first give you a condensed version of the story behind my ascent to Malaysia.

Was scouted and then hired by Ogilvy & Mather Direct, Los Angeles.

In 1985, I was working in my home state of Minnesota as a copywriter for a Minneapolis advertising agency called Colle & MeVoy.

Moved from my home state of Minnesota to L.A. by car. I wanted to keep my Honda Accord. God knows why. (But it was a darn good car.)

Took 3 days to get to L.A.

Found an apartment in Westwood. Yeah, yeah, I know. Anyone who knows L.A. knows that Westwood, the home of UCLA, is infested by the upwardly mobile. Michael J. Fox lived there, I'm told, before his rise to sitcom star status. And I do admit to bumping into several celebs, some major, some minor. The pinnacle of sightings, to me, was Mel Torme, who jumped ahead of me as I waited to buy movie tickets (there were, I believe, 12 cinemas within walking distance of my apartment). Oh, in case you are going "Mel who?", he's the guy who wrote and sang The Christmas Song ("Chestnuts roasting on an open fire …").

Anyway, he said, "Oh, sorry, did I jump ahead of you?" I said, "Yes, but not a problem." He smiled. A pause. Then I said, "I'm a great admirer of your work. You are such a talented man." He said, "Thank you", and smiled again. We both ambled up to the ticket office. I actually, well half-actually, expected him to buy a ticket for me, for the jumped queue mistake. But he bought his own ticket, turned to me and said, "Enjoy the show".

It turned out to be a lousy movie. Mel left halfway through. But he was carrying a brown, battered briefcase. And to this day, I wonder what was in it.

But I digress again.

I was hired after a paid trip to Chicago for a personal interview with the Creative Director, complete with dinner and a rather poncey 5-Star hotel; and another paid trip to L.A. with a stay at a Rodeo Drive hotel, in Beverly Hills, plus interviews with the existing L.A. direct marketing staff.

My O&M experience in L.A. is an entirely different book of its own. But I will tell you this. The Creative Director, who was based in San Francisco, presented the first new business pitch I was involved with at O&M Direct L.A. She was stunning in an outfit she told us had just been purchased on her recent trip to Italy. It was a purple leather outfit, an ensemble of jacket, blouse and mini-skirt. Perhaps, "stunning" is a mild description. Simply put, it was SO L.A. and set the tone for the days to come.

From O&M Direct L.A. came O&M Direct Hong Kong. Again, there is a novel in-between. And someday, when my lawyers agree to it, it will be published.

But I ended up in Hong Kong, because, according to O&M's worldwide creative godsend at the time, someone was needed there. And there I went. My first step out of America.

I was transferred with the title: Regional Creative Resource.

So while they needed help in Hong Kong, any office that needed help could call on me. That included the Philipines, Thailand, Indonesia, Singapore, Bangkok, Taiwan or Kuala Lumpur. Did my bit in Hong Kong for a while, then received a call for aid in Malaysia.

And there I went. The folks in Hong Kong were not very helpful about what I was to expect in Malaysia. I had spent less than a year in Hong Kong, and was still reeling from my first image of the city upon leaving the airport and heading for the taxi stand.

My first local Hong Kong view, keeping in mind this is my first trip out of America, was of an elderly Chinese man, emptying his nose by holding one nostril and then blowing. The other nostril emptied quickly, and largely, onto the waiting pavement. It was my welcome vision to Hong Kong.

To Malaysia I went, answering the call. This was 1987. No computers. No managing director. A staff of 5. (A division within an agency of 150 or so.). The singular Direct Marketing client: American Express. I did a couple of rescue missions to Malaysia before I offered myself full-time. It's simply a nicer place to live and work. I became the Creative Director of O&M Direct Malaysia.

I'm proud of my 5 years stay at O&M Direct KL, (now called OgilvyOne). Carol Champagne, who became the MD of our division, and I, managed to forge a pioneering Direct Marketing movement that has since become, nearly, commonplace. Now Direct Marketing, including CRM, is increasingly regarded as an essential element of smart profit-building strategies.

Yes, indeed, we were at the start of it all, here in Malaysia. We set the standard, we won the country's first international Direct Marketing awards and we made money. Now I am a partner with Drayton Bird, Crocker & Mano Sdn Bhd, an advertising and direct marketing agency, and have been living in Malaysia full time since 1989.

So what does this have to do with the rest of the world? Well, see for yourself. What follows is a collection of articles I've written since I've been here. All were published in a widely distributed regional marketing magazine called ADOI. Look for the differences in your own experiences, if you like. Or, look at the similarities.

I've also included snippets about Malaysia that include food, where you could live in KL and what that would be like, the current night-life and possible excursions from the capital city to elsewhere. And perhaps a few surprises.

If, after reading this book, you regret buying it, too bad. Money spent is my money earned. If, however, you enjoy it, make me happy. Send me a message. Love to hear from you.

All the best,

Kurt Crocker
kcrocka@gmail.com

Requiem for a Direct Marketing Heavyweight

Author's note: This was written shortly after the death of David Ogilvy, one of advertising's most notable icons. I offer it to you as a prologue to this book.

One of David Ogilvy's biggest regrets was that he took his agency public. That led the way for WPP and a new, but not necessarily improved, financially-driven corporate culture at Ogilvy & Mather. David was not amused, despite the bundle he made from the deal.

O&M may or may not be returning to their roots, but one thing is certain. The foundation from which David built his agency remains as sure and steady today as it was some 50 years ago. A foundation formed, in no small way, by his "his first love and secret weapon": Direct Marketing.

From the very beginning, David used Direct Marketing strategies to identify prospects who were interested in his clients' products and services. He knew that, at the very least, Direct Marketing could be a powerful way to generate leads.

Later he realized that Direct Marketing could also help his clients keep customers longer and make them more profitable. He knew he needed specialists for that, and bought the expertise to set up a Direct Marketing division in his New York office ... long before his competitors got around to it.

In a speech to Direct Marketing specialists in London years ago, David identified a few other milestones that helped himself, his agency and his clients profit:

- At the age of 25, he went to work as an office boy for Mather & Crowther in London and took a correspondence course in Direct Mail, which he paid for himself.

  When a client prospect — with an ad budget of £100 — dropped in, he was passed off to the office boy. The client had bought a country house and was about to open it as a hotel. David spent the budget sending postcards to everyone living near the hotel. Six weeks later when the hotel opened, it was fully booked.

- When David first started Ogilvy & Mather in New York, the agency was unknown. Within a few months they were growing so fast they had to turn down new accounts. During that time he had sent personalized mailings to the manufacturers who were their prospects. A great many of these prospects became attracted to the agency because of the mailings.

- He sold $750,000 executive jets for Cessna by "delivering mysterious cartons to the offices of some industrial big shots". The cartons contained homing pigeons, with a memo saying, "If you would like a test flight in a Cessna Citation Jet, release me." David noted that some of the big shots killed the pigeons and ate them, "but a lot released them and they flew home, with the address of the prospect strapped to their legs."

Even David's famous "Man in the Hathaway Shirt" ads contained elements of Direct Response. He wrote the original ad using a fairly generous amount of copy, nothing less than required to sell the product. That's the first rule of Direct Response.

And at the end of the ad, David included a clear call to action, with a means to respond: "At better stores everywhere, or write C.F. HATHAWAY, Waterville, Maine, for the name of your nearest store. In New York, telephone OX 7-55566. Prices from $5.95 TO $20.00."

David was truly a man of vision, in the fullest meaning of that overused and often undeserved accolade. He was also a gentleman.

He sent me a hand-written postcard when I first joined Ogilvy & Mather Direct in Los Angeles back in 1985, with a few words of friendly advice and a picture of Touffou, his castle-home in France. We corresponded occasionally until a few years before I left O&M KL in 1995 to form Drayton Bird, Crocker & Mano. David was willingly ready with praise, encouragement or a succinct and relevant suggestion.

It was heartbreaking to see him step aside to watch the money-handlers begin to transform the child he had given birth to and nurtured for so many years. Or course, it was even sadder to hear he had left us all forever.

But David's passion for Direct Marketing was an early and lasting impression, and why I have been and remain one of its most ardent advocates. For that, I will always be grateful.

You do WHAT for a living?

Crocker's my name. Direct Marketing's my game.

Huh?

Normal folks - the people who believe marketing is a shopping trip for groceries - get all glassy-eyed when I tell them I'm a Direct Marketer. ("You mean you go *directly* to the grocery store?")

But even those wild and crazy people in the ad biz sometimes blur. In fact, one hot shot marketing exec once asked me, "Yeah, you do Direct Marketing. But do you do CRM?". And believe it or not, this guy had regional responsibilities for Direct Marketing.

(For the uninitiated, CRM, or Customer Relationship Management, is an integral part of the Direct Marketing process. To be a Direct Marketer without CRM expertise could be likened to a spouse unable to consummate a marriage. Needless to say, I was shocked and appalled by the guy's question.)

So as a primer for those not in-the-know - or who should be in-the-know but aren't - I'll start with an overview. There are, broadly, three things a Direct Marketer does for a living:

1. Find customers
2. Keep customers
3. Make customers more profitable

Now let's take it step by step ...

Find Customers. Advertising is a marketer's attempt to find customers. It represents a fervent hope that a prospect will remember the brand and, soon thereafter, buy it.

Direct Marketers also use advertising - in virtually all media - to build brand awareness and increase sales. But with a twist. With Direct Marketing, there is a direct measurement of a prospect's response to the advertising.

A Direct Marketer may want a prospect to become a customer immediately, and offer him or her an opportunity to purchase a product "off the page". That is, to complete a coupon built into the advertising, give up some credit card information, and request direct delivery. Or call a toll-free number and do the same with an operator who will complete the order.

Direct Marketers also use a two-step process to find customers. For example, we might ask a prospect to request more information, especially if the product is expensive or complicated. Then, follow up with the prospect through a mailing or sales call.

If a prospect doesn't become a customer after step two - and it is believed he or she could still become one - more follow-up steps are added to the process. A Direct Marketer will take as many additional steps to convert a prospect into a customer as are economically feasible.

We also find customers by other means. A mailing targeted to a consumer profile deemed to be likely prospects is one of these other means. A website that offers an opportunity to request information or updates via e- or land-mail is another. There are more.

Keep Customers. A Direct Marketer's job should not stop with the happy conclusion of a prospect/customer conversion. The ultimate marketing objective would be that once you acquire a customer, that customer never buys a competitive brand again. While this may not be totally obtainable, you can at least aim for the purchase of your brand more often than not.

Again, a Direct Marketer's strategic approach to this objective depends on the potential return-on-investment. That's a little easier to do if you first determine the lifetime value of a customer. Then it's a matter of designing communication opportunities that - in some form or another - encourage continued loyalty to your brand.

A Direct Marketer engenders loyalty in many ways. A simple "thank you" after a measured first-purchase is always a good idea, and one of the easiest to accomplish. Clubs often work, especially if they are linked to sales. A series of communications, consistently offered with relevant content, can be effective ... even if they are not purchase-driven. There are more.

Make Customers More Profitable. Let's assume you are fairly confident that a customer is favorably impressed with your brand. You know he or she has purchased your Product A and likes it. Why not offer a "+" accessory and turn your customer's purchase into Product A+.

Or let's say you know that a lot of customers who bought Product A also bought your Product B. Just look into your database for Product A buyers. Select the ones who have not yet purchased Product B and send them information and an offer for this complementary cross-sell.

With upgrades and cross-sells, a marketer benefits through greater and continued profits. But these tactics can also build overall brand loyalty. That's especially true with financial institutions with a portfolio of services: the more relationships a customer has with a bank, the less likely he or she is to shop around for other financial solutions.

This 3-Stage Process - find customers, keep customers, make customers more profitable - is what Direct Marketers do for a living. And, yes, when you keep customers and make them more profitable, you are managing customer relationships. CRM. The nice bits beyond the nuptials (in case you didn't know).

"I wanna grow up to be a Direct Marketer"

Y ou parents hear it as a matter of routine, don't you?

Auntie visits you for tea, biscuits and the latest family gossip. She spies the little ones and miraculously breaks them from their latest computer game reverie with the question, "And what do you want to be when you grow up?".

Their inevitable answer, "I wanna be a Direct Marketer."

You smile and think to yourself proudly, "Of course you do, darling." Forget about the perks of having a doctor or lawyer as a progeny. Your kids will have the entire world at their feet!

Ok, I'm awake now. It's not that growing up to be a Direct Marketer won't earn you fabulous riches and global fame. It can. It has.

One Direct Marketer I know of, who specialised in securing subscribers for countless magazine titles, earned enough to enjoy the good life in a luxurious apartment on Russian Hill, overlooking the San Francisco Bay.

Another is a landed gentry living outside of London, who has the option (on whatever whim) to spend time by the fireplace, cognac in hand, at his quaint little cottage in France.

There are many more examples of Direct Marketers who live the lifestyles of the Rich and Famous. But let's face it. No one, anywhere, pins his or her hopes of a gloriously successful future on the goal of entering the world of Direct Marketing.

How come? Well, for one thing, it's not exactly running on a professional education stream. You can dream to get your Masters in Business. Or Marketing. Or Advertising. Or even Public Relations, for crying out loud. But not even in America, where Direct Marketing began with a mail order business called Sears & Roebuck, can you aspire to obtain your professional degree in Direct Marketing.

So from where do Direct Marketers spawn?

I graduated with a B.A. in Journalism, but landed my first job as a copywriter at Fingerhut, one of the world's biggest mail order companies. (No, it doesn't sell massage products.) I never looked back. Direct Marketing is my life.

One of the most talented Direct Marketers I ever hired walked into my office holding a résumé that noted his recent graduate work at Berkley. His thesis-in-progress was on Joseph Conrad. (Inexplicably, after years in the discipline, he decided to take up painting.)

But most who become Direct Marketers cut their teeth in either the business world or advertising agencies. That can be good or bad, depending on what baggage they carry.

It takes some time to wrap one's mind around the process and practices of Direct Marketing. A mindset elevation must occur that moves the goal of acquiring customers towards a devotion to owning them. That's not easy for those who have always concentrated on the single sale. Or for Brand Managers who narrowly define success – meaning a promotion and pay raise – as achieving short-term sales goals. A good, but limited vision.

But advertisers and advertising agencies will remain the likely birthplaces of Direct Marketers for some time to come. Copywriters and Art Directors will also find their way to Direct Marketing from less interesting homes at newspapers and design shops.

So we're not likely to overhear kids wistfully imagining themselves as a grown-up Direct Marketing professional anytime in the near future. And perhaps that's ok. As long as the best and brightest of them eventually see the light and evolve.

"You've been living so long in Malaysia. What do you miss about America?"

I get that a lot. Now I usually reply: "Season changes."

Even when I lived in Los Angeles, the city offered subtle seasonal climate changes. Warm to hot days and mostly cool nights (never used an air conditioner there for sleeping) but also a rain and wind season. There are monsoon seasons in Malaysia, so I guess that sort of counts.

My home state of Minnesota, however, is the mother of all seasonal severities. I emphatically do not miss Minnesota winters, but love Spring, Summer and Autumn there.

During my early years in Malaysia, I answered the question with "Choices". I missed the choices I had in American supermarkets.

In the early 90's, Malaysian grocery markets, from this American's perspective, were very basic. Single, lonely brands of cereals and ice cream. Just a couple selections of toothpaste, tissue or shaving cream. Canned soup was essentially cream of tomato or mushroom.

Then came the Giants and Cold Storages; big super and hyper markets that provide a wide variety in every isle. Australian beef has been added to local choices, and in the last few years, U.S. beef as well. (There was a brief ban after the Mad Cow scare.) Still not quite up to the standards of U.S. Midwestern-grown beef, though.

Even the shopping carts (ok, trolleys) have become bigger.

So what do I miss now about America? Sticking to the food theme, I would say American Breakfasts (they're just not the same here), especially potato pancakes. The glorious rib eyes my sister buys from a butcher in a tiny farm town called Concord. Or, better, The Minnesota State Fair. Deep fried cheese curds. Pronto Pups. Pork Chops on a Stick.

In other words, the only thing I really miss is being within hugging distance of my sister and long-time friends. And that's a very big deal, indeed.

Top Ten "Most Wanted"

T he Most Frequently Heard Questions and
Comments About Direct Marketing in Malaysia

When I first arrived in Malaysia nearly 20 years ago, not a whole lot of folks were asking specifically about Direct Marketing. Within a couple of years, however, there were many questions and comments. And today, I keep hearing them again and again.

I'm not sure what that signifies, exactly. There has been a tremendous increase here in the level of awareness of Direct Marketing as a discipline, and as a hard-working marketing tool. Yet the same questions and comments persist.

In the style of David Letterman (his show is no longer broadcast here – gee, I miss him so) I offer you: My Top Ten list of most heard questions about and perceptions of Direct Marketing ... along with my replies:

Number 10: "It's too expensive!"

This is an especially fun comment when made by a Marketing Manager who's spending millions on advertising. Does this guy know, I wonder, whether or not the money he's investing in his multi-million ringgit ad campaigns is wisely spent? If there has been marginal or unquantified return, then couldn't one argue that his campaigns may have been "too expensive". Alas, traditional forms of communication are often simplistically rationalised, and advertising budgets rarely questioned.

You don't have to spend a huge amount of money to test the power of Direct Marketing. Start small, if you must. But start, and start wisely, with the help of Direct Marketing specialists. Then, when you see the results, ask your experts how you can use Direct Marketing to its fullest potential.

Number 9: "Can you guarantee results?"

With Direct Marketing, you should always be able to guarantee a measured response. If you're an expert in the discipline, you should also be able to guarantee that your knowledge and experience will combine to create the greatest possible success.

Can you guarantee that the effort will always be profitable? No. But if your product or service, distribution network, sales force and customer service capabilities are all solid, the chances for success are very high. But again, you must rely on specialists.

Number 8: "No one reads long copy."

"Long copy" is very often associated with Direct Marketing. A lot of direct response press ads use long copy. Mailings sometimes have long letters - one charity mailing I read once had a 12-page letter (it was their "control" mailing, and generated huge donations). DRTV is usually longer than traditional television commercials.

John Hegarty, Chairman of Bartle Bogle Hegarty, quoted Oscar Wilde in a April 2000 ADOI magazine interview: "My apologies for this letter being so long. Had I more time it would have been shorter." John's point about "unchecked verbosity" is an excellent one.

A poorly written long copy ad or letter will fail against well-written short copy. No one wants to wade through "unchecked verbosity". However, in Direct Marketing, copy length should be dictated by what you are trying to achieve.

If you are asking someone to reply for free information, shorter copy will do. If your product or service is complicated or expensive, and you want someone to make a direct purchase or at least a firm commitment, long copy is a must.

But you must be interesting, logical and persuasive. And long copy must use short words, short sentences and short paragraphs, with plenty of crossheads to highlight benefits-at-a-glance.

Number 7: "No one reads junk mail in Malaysia"

No one reads junk mail anywhere. Except, perhaps, the very lonely. Junk mail has been defined as "the wrong message to the wrong person at the wrong time." That's the mail that gets glanced at and thrown directly in the bin where it belongs.

The best way to turn junk mail into desired mail is to choose your recipients carefully. Your list is by far the most important factor in predicting the success or failure of a mailing, so precise targeting is essential.

But are Malaysians somehow culturally pre-indisposed to receiving sales messages through the mail? No. There are plenty of local examples that prove Malaysians are as receptive as anyone, anywhere to direct mail. Consumer mail order is becoming a multi-million ringgit business here, and business-to-business mailings have been delivered with great success.

Number 6: "Do we really need a letter in our direct mail package?"

The letter is probably the most inexpensive element in any direct mail package. And yet, it's too often not included. Letters are sometimes "faked" by including them on the inside cover of a catalog or brochure. Bad idea.

A good sales letter should make the difference between a lukewarm response and a hot one. It's the only "personal" element in the package, ostensibly written by a named human being - from one person to another. The more personal you can make it, the better it will be.

You should consider the letter your "salesperson", the brochure your "store". Would you try selling something in your store without a salesperson? Unless your product or service completely sells itself, never send out direct mail without a letter.

Number 5: "I've heard 2% is a good response. Right or not?"

Sure, if you target 100,000 prospects and you need sales from 2,000 respondents to make a profit on your campaign investment, then 2% is fine. A good response rate is inextricably linked to your margins, cost of promotion and the number of people you are targeting. You may need a fraction of a percentage to make money. Or much higher response rates for expensive campaigns or slow moving products.

In other words, that magic 2% you hear so much about is nonsense. If someone says otherwise, run like the wind and look for another "expert".

Number 4: "We need Direct Marketing specialists. But my agency handles 'above line'."

Any communication created mainly to generate response should be the domain of Direct Marketing specialists. That could include direct mail, plus television, press ads, radio, outdoor, websites ... the full spectrum of communication channels.

Generalists will not know the many techniques used to get a prospect's immediate commitment or measured interest. A responsive television or press ad, for example, should be extraordinarily different in form and content than simple brand advertising.

So forget those lines, below or above. Think about what you are trying to accomplish, and employ the right people to do the job.

Number 3: "How long does it take to put together a Direct Marketing campaign?"

Responsive press takes about as much time as brand press. Television may require a little more production or post-production time, because the length of a DRTV spot is usually between 60 and 120 seconds.

Direct mail will require the longest lead-time, especially if you have names to source, a lot of personalisation or many elements. Someone once figured there are more than 100 steps required to complete a Direct Mail package ... or about 100 opportunities to screw up.

A totally integrated Direct Marketing campaign is quite a balancing act, and another reason to allow a single specialist resource to handle everything. As a rule of thumb (and this could vary wildly, depending on the communication mix) allow at least 6 to 8 weeks from start to launch date.

Number 2: "We've never done Direct Marketing. I don't know where to begin."

First, think of Direct Marketing as just another form of advertising, like brain surgery is another form of medical practise. Don't worry about where, when or how Direct Marketing will work best for you. Just put together a sensible brief, clearly identifying any relevant background information and your current objectives.

Review this brief with a Direct Marketing expert, allow some time for him to come back with a plan, and listen to the recommendations. A good plan will include advice about what you need in place before, during and after the campaign.

For advice about who to talk to, see Number 1 below ...

Number 1: "How many agencies do Direct Marketing in Malaysia?"

There are a handful who truly do have the depth of knowledge, people and experience to include Direct Marketing as a specialist discipline. The rest acknowledge that they do not offer such capabilities, or they say they do but really don't.

To separate the wheat from the chaff, ask the agency that claims Direct Marketing expertise the following questions:

1. What Direct Marketing campaigns have your agency worked on, and what were the results? (Look for experience and strong results in a broad range of product categories.)
2. Who are the people who will work on my Direct Marketing campaign, and what are their specialist backgrounds? (And then meet and talk with them.)
3. Is 2% a good response rate? (If they say yes, walk out the door.)

How to Embrace Your Cheatin' Heart

Your cheatin' heart will make you weep
You'll cry and cry and try to sleep
But sleep won't come the whole night through
Your cheatin' heart will tell on you

Hank Williams
"Your Cheatin' Heart"

I've always believed that the relationship between a client and his agency ought to be like a happy, monogamous marriage. They should walk together, hand in hand, on a mutually beneficial path toward the contentment of ever-increasing sales. As long as they both shall live.

And there are clients who have stood by their agencies for decades. Those long-lasting relationships have created mighty brands, often through the symbiotic nurturing that only time and intimacy allow.

Sadly, marketing couplings that can celebrate anniversaries beyond a single decade are exceptions to the rule. Like marriages of the human kind, agency/client divorce rates are very high.

There are many reasons why clients leave their agencies, but most of them are pretty lame. So you had a bad year, so what? Work it out together; you're a team! You didn't reach your goals? Don't just point fingers at your partner; search and destroy the bad as one and create a brighter future!

More often than not, clients should stick with their agencies through thick and thin. Then again, sometimes there can be made a very strong case for an extramarital fling. Even, let's say, an on-going, long-lasting affair on the side.

Let's face it. There are circumstances when certain agencies simply cannot provide what their client partners need. The inadequacy may be painfully obvious - "You're just not big enough for me." But usually the situation is more subtle, a lingering undercurrent ... the need to be truly satisfied.

Some advice to all clients yearning for more: couples therapy is not required. Go ahead and continue your current relationship. But be honest. Tell your agency what you are going to do and then do it. Begin that long-lasting affair.

Research has discovered that 9 out of 10 clients feel unfulfilled with their agencies because they have not experienced the orgasmic joy of working with true Direct Marketing professionals.

OK, I made that up.

But figure it out. Without Direct Marketing and CRM, measuring success is too often downright airy fairy. Clients miss out on the excitement of immediate response and results they can see, hear, touch. And they never experience the pulsating joy of creating and nurturing profitable customer relationships, long-term.

If your agency doesn't have a Direct Marketing division, or worse by far, passes off commoners as DM/CRM experts, the selling process is either woefully limp or simply a fraud. Now that's the ultimate deceit: faking it.

Your agency wants (or ought to want) you to be happy. So let them in on your plans to get up close and personal with Direct Marketing and all its seductive powers. (It's not cheatin' if you're honest about it.)

A guarantee. Contrary to Hank Williams' prediction, you won't cry and cry. In fact, yours will be the biggest smile in the room. And your envious fellow marketers will want what you're having.

Wandering in Malaysia

There are many things to do and see in and around Kuala Lumpur. It's a fairly typical, large Asian city, so expect the usual shopping, dining and nightlife experiences.

The uniqueness of KL is really about its culture and food, but there are also architectural monuments like the Petronas Twin Towers and KL Tower in city central. I always take visitors to a restaurant/hostel called The Coliseum, a charmingly grungy colonial-aged eatery that specializes in sizzling steak. I'm convinced some of the waiters have been there for all of its 87 years.

Chinatown in KL is interesting. There's a fabulous noodle shop tucked behind the man frying crispy pancake deserts in a huge shallow wok. Look for him or you'll miss it.

Batu Caves is a 20-minute drive from central KL. This Hindu shrine is a straight, 272-step walk up into 3 huge limestone caves. Quite a journey in tropical heat and humidity, but my sister did it and so can you.

Drive south for about an hour to the city of Melacca, a place the Chinese, Dutch, Portuguese and British each once claimed its own. Again, the food! But check out Jonkers Street if you like antiques, and visit the Baba Nonya museum, which is a house as it would have been long ago.

A few of my more wilderness-whacky visitors have traveled the 4-hour bus ride and 3- to 4-hour boat ride to reach Malaysia's interior ... and one of the world's oldest rainforests. The prospect of jungle leeches has dampened by desire for the experience.

Instead, I prefer to drive north, to Penang Island, with a mandatory rest stop in Ipoh at the 102-year old F.M.S. restaurant. In Penang, it's The Lone Pine Hotel, the first hotel built on Batu Ferringhi Beach. And, there, I head for one of the netted hammocks tied between two towering casuarina trees and let the sea breeze and sunset take over.

POP QUIZ: Test Your DMIQ

I used to have nightmares when I was attending college. In one, I would walk into a lecture hall for the first time and discover the class was already through the first of half of the semester. Mid-term papers due today. Sound familiar?

I would wake up in a cold sweat, only to remember I was but a few chapters behind in a couple of marketing classes. Gloriously relieved, I would head off to class, chain up my trusty ten-speed, wander into the lecture room and find my seat.

Inevitably, the Nazi war criminal disguised as my professor would smile sardonically and present us with ... a pop quiz. Naturally, the quiz concerned the chapters I had yet to read.

Well, it's pay-back time. Here's one on Direct Marketing, the answers to which cleverly appear upside down at the end of this chapter. But no headstands are allowed while taking the quiz ... only after.

Q1:   What is the ideal number of elements in a Direct Mail Package?

A) Two   B) Three   C) Five   D) As many as it takes

Q2:   What is the most important element of a Direct Mail Package?

A) Outer Envelope   B) Letter
C) Brochure   D) Response Device

Q3:   What is the most important influence on the success of a Direct Mail Package?

A) Offer   B) List   C) Timing   D) Creative

Q4:   Why do most businesses lose customers?

A) Product dissatisfaction   B) Customer moved away (or died)
C) No contact from the business   D) Competition

Q5:   What's considered a good response (orders or enquiries) in a Direct Marketing programme?

A) 2%   B) 2.5%   C) 5%
D) What ever it takes to at least break even

Q6:   Which medium has been shown to achieve the greatest "spontaneous awareness"?

A) Press   B) Television   C) Direct Mail   D) Radio

Q7:   In a 90-second Direct Response Television Commercial, what is the minimum time a toll-free number should appear on-screen?

A) 5 seconds   B) 10 seconds   C) 20 seconds   D) 30 seconds

Q8: Research indicates that web surfers read a screen at what percentage of normal reading speed?

A) 28%   B) 52%   C) 74%   D) 100%

Q9: Can you sell complex products online? How much - per month - would you guess one U.S. company has made in internet sales of new and used cars?

A) $2 million   B) $10 million   C) $50 million   D) $300 million

Q10: Which of the following is NOT a reason why people don't buy online?

A) No pre-sale assistance on-site   B) No purchase instructions
C) Fear of credit card security   D) No details about product availability

SCORING YOUR DMIQ

1-3 correct	Attend a good Direct Marketing seminar at your earliest opportunity (Or keep reading this book ... cheaper, lah.)
4-6 correct	You are emerging from the dark ages. Pursue your evolution.
7-9 correct	Have we met before?
10 correct	Are you standing on your head? If not, you're hired.

Lies About Size

It's remarkable what we ad agency types are willing to blurt out for public consumption. Sometimes it's merely brag and boast. Too often, it's just absurd.

I am not completely untouchable in this area. Back in my days at O&M, we approached new business prospects with the promise of what was then called "orchestration". I thought it a lovely word to replace the rather cold and calculated alternative: "integration". The equally cold, and frustrating, fact-of-the-matter was that whatever it was called, it really didn't exist.

I'm sure O&M is doing this "total communications" thing better now, as are all the other big, international agencies (yeah, right). But back then, my Direct Marketing division at this esteemed global entity (I was in love with David Ogilvy then, and still am, god rest his talented soul) was pretty much left to succeed or fail on its own.

So, in reality, we were a mini, specialist agency, tucked beneath the corporate armpits of an elder- and rather distant - cousin. Those days, as they say, we were a team of five at the earliest stages. Yet, we peddled ourselves as part of gigantic and completely synergistic machine, therefore completely able to deliver our one-on-one, long-term relationship solutions.

The truth was that we were capable of delivering those solutions without the corporate armpit. And, more often than not, we did.

DBC&M, my current interest, is also a small agency. And "big is better" is still the battle cry of our people-endowed, network-connected counterparts. But predictably, I suppose, that battle cry can become desperately vindictive.

Some of these big agency types will say absolutely anything to meet their HQ's profit projections. One of these agency types, I'm told, suggested to Client X that Agency X should not be a considered choice because Agency X was "too small and couldn't possibly handle the business". This is an example of the aforementioned absurdity. Even the biggest agencies can't "handle the business" if they don't have a willing, caring, dedicated and knowledgeable team. Frankly, too many of them don't.

And let's get back to this "global resources" claim. I can count on one finger the number of times I took advantage of O&M's much-touted worldwide network. (For the record, O&M is not the employer of the agency type just mentioned. I have many friends there still and I'm very proud of them.) If you have international knowledge, and can knowledgeably apply it to the local market, you really don't need a global network.

There's more about the bigness issue. Imagine a huge, international Direct Marketing agency that talks about global resources here in Malaysia, promises full service but declines to reveal staff-on-hand. Why not simply say, "Yes, we're small now. (Or even, "we don't have any staff to speak of yet.") But as we grow we will help our clients enjoy greater sales. And we have the expertise to do that."

Why the lies about size? Because, somehow, "bigness" has replaced "service and solutions" as a selling point. Perhaps it's time for agencies like mine to resurrect the old, and beautiful, Volkswagen battle cry: "Think Small."

Murder Most Faux ... the "Direct Marketer" Did It

It wasn't real. It never was.

Even so, the price had been paid. Or, at least, billed. Payment was another matter altogether. The agency lads could only hope for the best.

But I'm getting ahead of my story.

It all began one fateful day during a top-management meeting in a smoke-free conference room at the agency. As the debate continued to heat, the sun began to set, and coffee cups gave way to chilled lager and a less cautionary tone.

It wasn't about the awards, they agreed. It wasn't even about the work. It was, of course, about the money. About wanting more of it. For the agency. For themselves. And, oh yeah, for the staff. But how? Each had drawn their own map for a road to riches, and at this moment, their proposed paths had not intersected.

Creative billing? "Well of course, you dolt", someone snapped. "We've been doing that for years and where has it gotten us? A second company Merc and my move to Kenny Hills? Think big, ferchrissakes."

A New Creative Director? The suits groaned in common understanding. No words were needed to explain their disdain for breaking in another prima donna. It had taken three years to mold the current Creative "guru" into some form of obliging man-on-a-string. "Just do it" had finally been met with a nod, and they weren't about to start the process of debilitation all over again.

More client entertainment? "Hmmmm, yes, but selectively", another demurred. "Only for our mega-ringgit accounts. Even then, it's a long-term investment with no guaranteed income. It would strengthen the relationship, you say? Bull. It may be right, but we need right away."

As silence (save for a few lager inspired belches) befell the room, the most recent addition to this circle of power and decisiveness began a slow lean forward. The youngish exec loosened his Hugo Boss tie and nervously fidgeted with the Brietling chronograph he purchased as an investment in confidence. He cleared his throat with a soft "ahem" and began to speak.

"Here's a thought. We all know that more clients mean more money. And we've been pitching 'total communications' for quite some time. Trouble is, some buy it. Some don't. Maybe more would believe our 'integration' story if, um, er, well ... if we actually had a honest-to-goodness Direct Marketing division. You know, not just the team from PR? Or our creative group that handles all those corporate brochures? I'm mean a real, live Direct Marketing pro with a track record to prove it."

All the men at the table glared at the up-and-comer, their jaws dropped beyond the Windsor knot tied neatly ahead of starched Gucci collars. Then in unison, they broke into earsplitting guffaws, as beer spittle sprayed from nostrils and fat-fingered fists slapped the table in uncontrolled hysteria.

All the men did this, except one. The one sitting at the head of the table. When the laughter subsided, tears were wiped, and breathless utterances like "that's a good one" died down, the honcho at tablehead smiled gently and spoke.

"You do have a lot to learn, kid," he sneered. "But gentlemen, I think the fellow is on to something. No, we don't need a genuine Direct Marketing guy, my gawd, think of the expense. But we ought to be more genuinely convincing when we sell this 'total communication' thing to prospective clients. That's how we make more money, gentlemen. Now get me a body. Any body. Get him cheap. Package the crap out of him and stand him up when we pitch. Just do it. And do it now."

And so they did. And the business came. Budgets were approved. Projects began. The "Direct Marketing" guy proposed an ambitious and complicated mail campaign with words he borrowed from texts and promises he pulled from thin air. The client gave his go-ahead, sat back in confidence, and waited for the orders to pour in.

The orders didn't pour in. They didn't even trickle. The client disappeared. And, after threats from the demised client's boss, so did the "Direct Marketing" guy. Two careers murdered at the lick of several thousand misguided postage stamps.

But the "Direct Marketing" guy didn't really do it. The agency did. And they billed the client anyway.

The Story of Lori

When we started our agency, Drayton Bird, Crocker & Mano, in 1995, we set up space in a first floor office above a row of ground floor shops and restaurants. It was within walking distance from the offices of what was then our biggest client. And, ironically perhaps, it was also a walk away from the offices of Ogilvy & Mather, the alma mater of all the partners.

The area is very high traffic, with narrow roads and very little available parking. It's a triumph when you find an empty, legal curbside space after 15 minutes of circling.

Shortly after our start-up, I was reversing into one such space when I noticed a jam of cars stopped behind a large hauling truck on the thin road that separates two street-parking areas. I walked to the front of the truck to find a tiny ball of brown fluff, attempting to reach safer ground.

Except there was no safer ground. Even if this recently born pup reached the meridian, then crossed another lane of opposing traffic, it faced a road of cars searching for parking.

I sighed. Picked her up. Took the pup to the vet for a check-up and de-fleaing. Brought her home. And called her Lori, after the British term for truck. She's been with me since, so, what, around 13 years old? Lively and neurotic, but a bit deaf and arthritic.

Of course, the parking space was gone when I got back to the office.

Want Great Marketing Success?
Forget About Making Money

Forget about making money? Are we mad?

These days, more than ever, hearing those cash registers ring seems to be the single most important hope and dream of any business, big or small.

Every day, we ponder about cash flow. Profit projections. Return on investment. Debt management. It's taking care of business and it's about nothing but money.

Right? Well, yes, without money, you have no business. But think about that for a minute. Where does the money come from in the first place?

You make money if you have a product or service that's desirable enough to be purchased in volumes large enough for you to exceed breakeven costs.

But that's not marketing. That's Accounting 101.

Unfortunately, even in times when money's not as tight as it often is, the two disciplines are confused. Quite a few sellers of products and services, plus agency folks responsible for growing their brands, tend to use accounting mentalities when marketing decisions are called for.

Agency account managers amble into their clients' offices, marketing plans and creative concepts in hand, with petty thoughts on their minds. How much money will this plan earn for our agency? Is there enough high-margin advertising in the plan to earn the really big bucks? Will production costs for creative eat into our media budget? Will this agency plan help achieve revenue mandates set by our colleagues in Armani suits back on Madison Avenue?

OK, OK. That's not entirely fair. A few agency account managers actually amble into their clients' offices with the question, "Will this plan make money for my client?" But even that is the wrong question.

And, as they review the agency plans, clients have their own set of petty thoughts. Is this plan within budget guidelines? Am I getting the biggest bang for my buck? Where has the agency inflated estimates? (Sad to say, experience has earned them the justification for this question.) Or simply, will this earn me a raise and promotion?

OK, OK. That's also not entirely fair. A few clients actually respond to the agency's plans with, "Will this plan help sell my product?" But that's still the wrong question.

So what's the right question agencies and clients should be asking? If "how much profit will we make" isn't it, then what is? If the purpose of marketing is not about making money, what is the purpose?

The good Professor Theodore Levitt of Harvard Business School answered simply. He believed you should work above all "to make and keep a customer." And according to the British Institute of Marketing, marketing is all about "identifying, anticipating and satisfying customer requirements profitably.

Ah, you exclaim, there's that word ... profitably. Yes, but notice what's ahead of it. It's all about customer requirements.

No one is suggesting here that profits are undesirable. But if clients and agencies think more about customer requirements - and less about making money - chances are excellent they'll end up selling more products and services. And not just short term sales. Sales that will be more easily turned into long-term, mutually-beneficial customer relationships.

(This hints at a formula for agency success: Client Satisfaction = Satisfaction of Client's Customers = Greater Sales for Client + More Retained Accounts.)

"Profitably" should simply be an inward promise to deliver on customer requirements as cost-efficiently as possible. Greater marketing success is really all about how well you follow the golden rule of that Texas millionaire I often quote: "Find out what your customers need and want, give it to them, and get rich."

How can you apply this selfless, "consumer centric" and ultimately more successful thinking to your next campaign? A few ideas ...

Find out what your customers (or your client's customers) need and want through lead generation advertising - and fulfill their needs and wants by selling to them directly, or through delivery of information and offers that encourage purchase.

You can also communicate directly to a profile of prospects who are most likely to need and want your product or service. Or to a segment of your customers with likely needs and wants for a cross-sells or upgrades.

You can engender loyalty simply by saying "thank you" after a first purchase. And by communicating regularly to customers with information about new products, exclusive offers, special promotions. When done properly, a cycle of communication says a lot about how much you care about their relationship with you.

You can satisfy a need for "special treatment" by grouping high-value customers and reward them for greater purchase volumes.

These strategies, of course, scream for the inclusion of Direct Marketing in that aforementioned marketing plan. But after all, as my colleague Drayton Bird says, Direct Marketing is "one step closer to perfect marketing." And quite probably, your secret to greater marketing success.

Commonsense and the Jargonauts

W ords. Those ever-lasting words.

Well, sort of. In the worlds of Direct Marketing and advertising, we use a whole bunch of words. In fact, we are full of it. Er, them.

Some of the words we use make sense. I'm actually rather fond of "key targets" and "competitive frame" and "psychographics", two name a few.

But let's be honest with ourselves. We use many words that are simply empty-headed and invented-to-impress. Jargon. Words that go in and out of fashion like a Malaysian rainstorm during monsoon season, or remain to torment us like the heat.

Direct Marketing guru Drayton Bird, a man who has never been a jargonaut, gets positively English at the phrase "strategic marketing." That's been spewing from our mouths for decades. If it's marketing, shouldn't strategies be involved by definition? I should hope so.

One big shot agency once toyed with the words, "Differential Marketing." I hope they have given that plaything a rest. Because the word "Differential" is really just "Direct" on steroids.

Empowered by four syllables instead of two, "Differential" was intended sharpen the image of Direct Marketing fundamentals. Like dropping a synthetic toupee atop a handsome but hairless friend. But the bald truth is beautiful enough - yes, it's a good idea to "differentiate" individuals who will mostly likely buy your product or service. Why jargonize that?

The current Direct Marketing buzzword is CRM. Sorry, not a word. The current buzz-letters? The letters stand for Customer Relationship Management (or Marketing, as some prefer to explain the "M").

The only thing new about "CRM" is that more marketers are discovering its importance, and are more fully applying relationship management techniques. Technologies required for active CRM continue to grow more powerful and sophisticated.

CRM is, simply, a process to keep and increase the value of your customers - managed at every possible point of contact. Those three little letters label a broad range of marketing activities, including communications, list management, teleservices and the internet, among others.

Speaking of the internet, it has become the darling of Direct Marketers in America. As it should be. There is vast potential in identifying prospect interest, capturing direct sales, or fulfilling information requests through website homepages or site advertising. It's an opportunity many marketers in Malaysia have yet to exploit. But, predictably, jargon also flourishes in the cyberworld. (Cyberworld. There you go!)

"e-commerce" will one day make it in to Webster's, if it hasn't already. Not a bad piece of jargon, I suppose, but try starting a sentence with the damn thing. (See above. Looks a bit whimpy, don't you think?)

And read this, a quote from an article in the archives of dmnews.com: "Only a small percentage of the potential email universe is permission-based ... and as more and more people are opting out, extra pressure is being put on those who opted in ... "

Opt in. Opt out. Sounds like words edited from a sleazy romance novel with the side note "not quite as explicit as hoped". Get to the point. Want or not? And what's this "permission-based" and "email universe" nonsense? Few who receive email advertising actually request it. So say it!

It is true that advertising and direct marketing are in a constant state of evolution. Especially with the information explosion, and our ability to know more about customers and prospects than we've ever known before. But do we really need word-inventions to re-explain the fundamental facts-of-life?

Commonsense defeats the jargonauts. Guaranteed.

Above Line Bull and What To Do About It

T here's a smelly load of waste being thrown about the halls of advertising agencies and marketing departments. It's been thrown about for years. It's old. It's dangerous. It stinks. And it's time to stop.

This pile of bull is the outdated and empty-headed demarcation of "above-line" and "below-line" communications.

In the misguided extreme, "above-line" means any medium generally associated with traditional advertising. That would be television, press, radio, outdoor. "Below-line" means the rest: brochures and collateral, POS, and of course, direct mail.

Websites and other interactive media have, so far, maintained a category of their own. And that's wrong, too.

Above-line, below-line and interactive. The separatists imagine them as three distinct and dissimilar planets revolving around a shared star (the brand). In the galactic world of intelligent marketing, the brand ought to be at a planet's core, with all communications connecting to it through adjoining landmass.

In more graphic metaphorical terms, "above-line" and "below-line" is an antiquated bunch of crap. So how do you separate the wheat from this unwanted fecal confusion? (My, the metaphors abound.)

Specifically, how do you know when the specialised discipline of Direct Marketing should be employed in coordination with - or instead of - good old-fashioned advertising?

First of all, you must purge yourself of the ever-annoying misconception that Direct Marketing is only direct mail. Direct Marketing is just another form of advertising, one that uses the full range of communication possibilities.

Including press, magazines, television, even radio, outdoor and, yes, interactive media.

Secondly, you must ask yourself: "What is the main thing we are trying to achieve?"

Is the primary objective of your marketing programme to build the brand? Then do some advertising. Give the work to the generalists.

Or do you mostly want to encourage immediate action? A sale, now? An enquiry? Do you want your programme to increase memberships in a long-term loyalty programme? Do you want to interest, retain or reward the loyal customers your already have?

Do you want to achieve any or all of the above response-driven objectives *and* build your brand? Then do Direct Marketing. Give the work to the specialists.

And be sure your marketing mind is open to the possibilities of advertising, because that could very well be a tactic these specialists would recommend.

Direct Marketing specialists may suggest press and television advertising, for example, that include an option to respond directly (through phone, fax, website or coupon).

Or Direct Marketers may suggest an ad that speaks to a membership base, with say, a special offer or reward. Even though this sort of ad is only indirectly measurable, it belongs with the specialists - because it is part of your grand intention to reward and retain customers. And it will be best integrated with other tactics employed by those with the most vested interest in that objective - Direct Marketers.

When you allow Direct Marketing to fulfill its enormous potential through a variety of communication channels, you unleash an entire army, not just a wandering troop.

So please, let us at last cut the crap. Never say above- and below-line again.

Whatever food you fancy, you can find it in Malaysia.

Malaysia offers a multi-ethnically mixed choice of culinary delights. Malay, Chinese and Indian form the cultural roots of the food here, but there are also Eurasian influences plus Nyonya and the indigenous tribes of Borneo.

All local dishes offered in Malaysia should be considered Malaysian food. Malay food, however, is linked to the cultural and spiritual heritage of the Malay Islamic community.

One of the most famous Malay dishes is Nasi Lemak, which is a popular breakfast feast. Rice is cooked in coconut milk, the served wrapped in banana leaf with crispy anchovies fried in hot sambal sauce, cucumber slices, roasted peanuts and hardboiled egg. I've had this one plated with a curried drumstick on the side and, believe me, you won't need a mid-day meal.

Beef Rendang is another Malay dish widely enjoyed here. This one is cubes of beef braised with the flavours of coconut and hot spices and served dry. It is often accompanied by turmeric flavoured rice.

And every Malaysian foodie seems to have a best-ever recipe for Sambal Udang, a Malay sauce served with many local dishes. Smashed chilies, shallots, garlic, tomato and tamarind paste, plus a mandatory measure of dried shrimp paste called belachan, make up this tasty condiment.

The very first Malay food I sampled in Malaysia was Laksa, but it wasn't. There are different versions of Laksa in different parts of the country. The one I sampled was on a trip to Penang, and there it's called, you guessed it Penang Laksa. Unlike traditional "Malay" Laksa, the Penang version fish soup dish includes the sour flavour of tamarind, and is nicely stocked with shrimp and veggies.

Of course, if you are unadventurous, McDonald's burgers taste the same in Malaysia as they do everywhere else in the world.

More on Abolishing Above-The-Line

It's official, and has been for quite some time. Above-the-line advertising has been banned.

Also banned: Below-the-line "marketing activities".

And banned some more: Silly statements like "Web sites are really more about customer communication than Direct Marketing."

The phrase "above-the-line" has usually been applied to media opportunities. Above-the-line has meant advertising placed in newspapers and magazines, on radio, TV and outdoor boards. Essentially, above-the-line was meant to identify anything that reaches a relatively broad consumer audience, regardless of its marketing objective.

Some smart person, probably a Direct Marketing specialist, tried to dispel the myth of above-the-line communications by inventing another unhelpful phrase: "through-the-line". "Don't think 'above' or 'below'," he or she philosophised, "Think 'through'". Unfortunately, this theoretical approach does not directly address the fundamental practical question: "When should Direct Marketing specialists create advertising in media like press, magazines and TV?"

If "through-the-line" is to be useful jargon, let it mean the line that is drawn through all communications based on the questions: "Response or not? Now or later?" One might argue that all advertising should elicit some sort of response. Buy our product. Sign up for our service. Sales should be the prime directive for all marketing communications. But marketers don't always require an immediate response. Buy our product *now*. Sign up for our service *now*. Get more information *now*.

When response *now* is the main objective of your advertising, give it to a Direct Marketing specialist. Only they know all the techniques required to motivate immediate action, in any medium. Only Direct Marketing specialists are concerned with the totality of the selling cycle, from identification of prospects and customer acquisition, to maintaining and maximizing customer profitability.

"Above-the-line" be damned.

Damnation, also, to "below-the-line". Direct Marketing, which is so often mistakenly equated to Direct Mail, has been traditionally lumped with "below-the-line" activities like brochures, catalogs, take-ones and other point-of-sale material. And CRM, or Customer Relationship Management, is also deemed a "below-the-line" marketing activity, probably because it usually involves mailed (and/or emailed) communications.

This is wrong because it denigrates the purpose of Direct Marketing: To identify prospects and customers as individuals, and build lasting and mutually beneficial relationships.

Here's a consideration that contradicts the all-too-neat guideline: "Response or not? Now or later?" What if you have a Direct Marketing specialist managing your loyalty or rewards programme and you want a press ad to promote the programme's benefits? Not for the purpose of an immediate response; just to reinforce the participation of existing customers, and remind non-customers of what they're missing. Should your DM guys do the ad?

Yes. Because even though the ad is non-responsive, it is part of a long-term program that requires the delicate management of relationships. For the sake of both consistency and results, maintenance of those relationships mandates focused control. Keep your DM specialists at the helm.

As for Web sites, if your content and design are only about "customer communication", you are wasting your time and money. Your online efforts should realize every opportunity to turn prospects into customers, build your database and, at a minimum, offer existing customers a chance to interact with your brand. All of these objectives are only obtainable with the application of Direct Marketing principles.

"Web sites have little to do with Direct Marketing." Banned, banned, banned.

More on Malaysian food ...

As mentioned at the end of the last chapter, there is Malaysian food, and there is Malaysian Malay food.

There's also Malaysian Chinese and Malaysian Indian. Plus Malaysian Eurasian. And Nyonya. It's only complicated if you think too much about the origins, or the difference, say, between Malaysian Indian and Indian Indian dishes. Just eat and enjoy.

I used to frequent a restaurant located near the old international airport. There I first became acquainted with Chili Crab, a laborious but lovely eating experience and considered to be Malaysian Chinese.

A variety of generously sized crabs are wok-cooked, sizzling in chili sauce. They come to the table on a big platter, chopped in pieces to be sucked and picked at all night long. An icy cold beer is the perfect partner to Chili Crabs.

Noodles are an almost-daily meal in Malaysia, eaten at breakfast, lunch or dinner time. A favourite lunch treat of mine is Char Kway Teow, flat rice noodles stir-fried with shrimp, bean sprouts, egg and cockles. (No cockles for me, please.)

Malaysian Indian food is mostly about curry, and more curry. Eating at a "banana leaf" restaurant for the first time is quite a treat. A fresh, green banana leaf is set before you, on which is placed rice and your choice of curries and condiments. Eat with your hand (right hand only) or utensils if you must.

Nyonya food in Malaysia followed marriages between the first mainland Chinese settlers and their Malay brides. Many Malaysian Eurasian inspired foods have Portuguese influences, like Devil Curry, or Indian, like Pork Vindaloo.

Hungry for choice? Visit Malaysia.

The Perils of Pissy Partnerships

I would make a terrific client.

If I were a client, looking for an agency, I would first make a plan. I would ask myself, "What, exactly, am I looking for? What do I want an agency to do for me?"

If I were a client managing a significant brand, I would answer, "I'm looking for an agency to build my brand. And as the agency builds my brand, I want to maker greater and greater sales. Right now, and for a long time to come."

Shouldn't this be the goal of every major marketer? Heck, shouldn't it be the goal of every marketer, big or small? Even the owner of my neighbourhood mini-market should want to strengthen his brand and increase both short- and long-term sales. He is, like it or not, in competition with the Giants and Cold Storages of the grocery world - and has advantages he could and should exploit.

So if I were a client, I would look for an agency that could help me achieve these pure and perfectly attainable goals. I would ask, say, 6 agencies to show me how they've accomplished these goals for other clients. I would ask each of them to show me at least 3 case histories, including strategies and actual campaigns. I would want them to show me, over the course of a two-year or longer period, how they have strengthened brands and increased sales.

Then I would short-list the 6 agencies to 3 of the best. And, yes, I would ask them to compete with each other for my business. I would tell them all about my brand, about its history and its future. I would share my marketing objectives with each agency, and ask them to come up with a plan that would help me realize my goals. I would want at least a 1-year plan, with subsequent year contingencies. And creative work for each communication contact they may suggest.

The agency I choose would receive my business. The agencies that were short-listed but not chosen would receive at least RM10,000 for their considerable time and effort. They would also receive my sincere thanks, and a round of drinks for their team at a favourite watering hole. And I would expect my new agency to include me in their celebratory party.

The agency I choose would have employed all the necessary weaponry required to meet my goals. I would expect that to include the usual advertising and public relations guns, plus the powerful arsenal available through Direct Marketing, including customer acquisition and relationship management.

I would plan to stick by my agency through good times and bad, through sickness and health. That would take a lot of effort, by me and by my agency team, but that is the nature of partnerships. Clients and agencies should indeed have a loving and intimate relationship, one that is durable over time because of the mutual belief that they belong together.

It doesn't always work out that way, often because the people involved in sustaining the relationship change. But a client/agency union must rest firmly on the intention of lasting trust if any marketing effort they attempt together is to succeed.

If a client/agency relationship is anything less than a marriage, problems are almost guaranteed. Without a bond based on trust and respect, either partner is very likely to stray. Not just from a commitment to the brand, but also from the people dedicated to building it. The work becomes an assembly-line task serving faceless masters, rather than a marketing challenge solved by dedicated peers.

And forget project-by-project pitches. Handing out pitch briefs for, say, a brochure, with little promise of monetary reward, is not only financially implausible, it's counterproductive. Where does this task fit into the brand-building picture? A chosen agency responsible for the brand should not be held responsible for the potential damage that may be caused by "mistress" agencies. If you stray, you pay.

Not happy with your agency's communication plan, you say? The concepts presented were not quite right? Work it out. Explain precisely what you're looking for and go for a second round. Chances are that if you work closely together - and it may not be easy - you'll be delighted with the results.

If, try after try, your agency seems a hopeless cause, then make a clean break. Don't include them in a hopeless pitch. Cut your ties on a mutually agreed-upon schedule as you search for your new agency. But make sure you've tried everything before you end the marriage.

It takes a consistent effort over time to strengthen a customer's relationship to your brand. It takes the same commitment to create a rewarding relationship with your agency. Don't settle for anything less.

Direct Marketing in Three Acts

Methinks, sometimes, I have no more wit than a Christian or an ordinary man. But I am a great eater of beef and I think that does harm to my wit.

Those words, or something close to them, are the words of William Shakespeare as uttered by a character named Sir Andrew Aguecheek in Twelfth Night. Quite a few Malaysians had the chance to hear them spoken by yours truly some years back during Instant Café Theatre's production of that play. It was part of an Out in the Open arts festival held, well, out in the open on the grounds of the Carcosa Sri Negara colonial-style hotel. Queen Elizabeth has rested her weary royal head there during Comonwealth gatherings.

What on earth, you ponder, does the mention of a theatrical performance have to do with Direct Marketing? Nothing at all, I answer, if you think the theatre is nothing but a bunch of egomaniacal actors like myself making much ado about nothing. But if you think of theatre as a business, which it very much is here in Malaysia, than a specialised discipline like Direct Marketing could and should have a starring role.

In fact, I defy you to name a business category that could not employ the benefits of Direct Marketing. The only criteria necessary are the desire to make money and keep making money for some time to come. So let's look at the theatre as a business with those criteria.

Act One: *What's the situation in the theatre world here?*

A number of Malaysians have been paying to see stage productions for quite a few years now. But the number of Malaysian theatre-goers is relatively low, especially considering the many production choices that are now available. So while there is certainly no shortage of choices, it's quite a challenge to fill seats if you rely solely on a small group of existing theatrephiles.

The companies here that produce plays are varied. Some are very focused in the types of plays they offer; others are quite eclectic, offering everything from stand-up comedy and dance to original and classic plays.

The Actors Studio is a pioneer that began, as most theatre companies still operate, "floating" their productions from venue to venue. That is, most lease space from existing stage facilities for a pre-agreed period of time. Now Actors Studio has their own space, or spaces actually, staging productions from a theatre in the Kuala Lumpur "suberb" called Bangsar, and at the magnificent Kuala Lumpur Performing Arts Centre.

As for actors, there are very few who are full-time professionals. Salary standards are miserable. Training is limited. Incentives and pathways for choosing acting as a career are virtually non-existent, despite Malaysia's intentions of becoming a regional cultural hub.

Act Two:

Clearly, there is a need to expand the market size. But first, who is going to the theatre now? What is the profile of a typical Malaysian theatre-goer? And is the type of person who attends, say, an Instant Café Theatre production the same or different than one who regularly goes to an Actors Studio play? Or does the profile change from play to play regardless of the production company?

Once questions like these are answered, you will begin to see a much clearer picture of market prospects. A reliable profile of your current customers is mandatory if you want to attract more of the same. You will also discover segments within the whole that represent more reliable sources of revenue. That will help you market more intelligently to your current customers, as well as help you find new ones.

But if the theatre scene is to thrive, you must do more than just place bums in seats. The cost of leasing venues is not cheap, and even a company that has a resident venue has rent to pay.

Do the math. Say a typical "house" has 250 seats. A typical "run" is 12 performances. The average ticket price is RM35. Even with a full house every night (hardly ever happens) total ticket sales is RM105,000 ... tops. Add overheads like salaries and set production to venue expenses and it's easy to calculate the need for other revenue sources. Especially if the goal is to raise standards as well as curtains.

Act Three:

Expand Market Size. Let's assume that after serious rounds of profiling, we've determined that college-age students are an important prospect segment. Upper level executives in large companies is another. A Direct Marketing programme would cost-effectively target whatever high-value prospects you identify.

But if theatre companies are really serious about growing, they would do well to consider "lead generation" advertising, also a role for Direct Marketing. Create a campaign - funded by arts councils and/or the appropriate ministry? - solely designed to create a database of prospective theatre goers.

Most theatre companies currently use some form of Direct Marketing to communicate with their "existing" customers. I suggest, however, that current efforts are haphazard at best, and not very compelling or comprehensive. There are few who are taking advantage of opportunities to reward for loyalty, for example, or for getting their friends to the theatre.

Tap New Revenue Sources. Sponsorships and advertisers are an obvious need. Some companies have been all too regularly tapped by theatre companies and it's time to search for alternatives. Again, Direct Marketing has a role here, and it would not be just a one-off effort. To make a sponsorship/advertising programme even more cost-efficient you could also use a corporate base to sell tickets.

These are but a few opportunities for the local theatre scene if Direct Marketing got into the act in a more consistent and professional manner. And the same thinking could apply to any number of products or services. But I'm a great eater of beef, and it's time for lunch.

Direct Ideas about the Fourth Estate

W hat does a Direct Marketing guy like me do on a lazy Sunday morning? Why, muse over lost opportunities, of course.

Armed with a caffeine-laden cup of java, this is the usual routine: page through the people's paper for local, regional and world news, check in on the web slinger and that pizza loving cat, offer my verdict on the murdering matron, and peruse the press ads.

But it's the press ads that really get me going. That fact is, unless you're marketing a genuinely mass-consumed product, press advertising is very wasteful. You can figure safely that around 80% of the people who read newspapers don't give a hoot about what you're selling. And too many marketers never take the initiative to actually meet the few who are real prospects, or even marginally interested consumers.

Lost opportunities. Unless Direct Marketing saves the day.

Take Barley Leaf Extract, for example. Or any of the other nutritional supplements, organic or not. Now how many of you out there keep a good supply of these products at-the-ready? Not many, I venture. But a few do, and do religiously.

What a waste to simply advertise, when you could be asking these health-minded people to raise their hands and tell you who they are. Nutrition is an on-going concern for the few who care, and companies like Proviton or 21st Century or Thomson should be regularly communicating with them. Opportunity found: Lead generation press advertising and on-going direct mail to identified prospects.

How about adult diapers? Talk about a product that simply screams the desire for discretion. And I'm not at all denigrating the product's benefit. Adult incontinence is a serious problem that deserves a serious solution. But press advertising alone, without the possibility of future, discreet communications is a shame.

Why not offer a free booklet in the ad, say, "Living with Incontinence", and ask people to send for it via a coupon. Then plan to market to these people monthly, offering either direct-sale or perhaps home delivery by neighbouring retailers. What a convenience! What a relief! You'd be a hero and have a dedicated and thankful customer for life.

Or European travellers? I run around with people many would assume are jet setters. But not one in my gang regularly travels to Europe. We all know these frequent travellers are out there somewhere, and yes, they do probably read the Sunday paper. So if a travel agency is intent on advertising, advertise to get names, for crying out loud.

If you owned a travel agency, imagine what you could do with a good traveller database - your own proprietary list of prospects generated from press advertising. You could ask these people where they've travelled and when, and if they'd like to go there again. You could ask where they haven't gone and where they'd like to travel in future. You could ask them when they usually take a holiday, and when they start thinking about a destination.

With this information, you could communicate the right messages at the right times, by grouped individuals. You could even personalise offers.

Send a mailing in May - a travel planning kit - to people who say they start thinking about their travel destinations in June. Add a room upgrade offer to people who have told you that good hotel accommodation is a high priority when travelling. Or mail a promotional pack that visualises the sensual sights of Florence to everyone who's never been to Italy, or who has, and would like to go back.

These are but a few examples. Opportunities abound in practically every business category. Unfortunately, many of these opportunities are lost.

Ah well. I need another cup of coffee.

What To Do On A Sunday in Malaysia

I have a pretty boring routine on Sundays in Malaysia.

Usually, I will get up in time for a 20 minute drive to pick up Dita before 10 a.m. She's a live-in, full-time housekeeper/kid-minder who works for my friend Patrick Teoh. She and her employer have kindly agreed to allow me to borrow her services on Sundays, when she's available.

Laundry and housekeeping. But for the more adventurous, or self-tidy, there are many things to do on a reliably hot and humid Sunday in Kuala Lumpur.

Brunch is popular. But if you can get up earlier, say before 6 a.m., you could share a nice steaming pot of Bak Kut Teh with a few fellow sunrise devotees. Bak Kut Teh makes for a terrific breakfast or an after-pub/club supper and it's one of my all-time favorite meals.

It is also authentically Malaysian. This dish is pork, lovingly stewed in broth that is either soup-like or a tad thicker, depending on chef's preference. Every bit of the meat is deliciously tender and distinctly rich, and I'm told includes more than just the loin, if you know what I mean. Deep-fried, yet soft, bread-like bits are provided for dipping or adding into your personal bowl of this saucy wonder.

After this hearty breakfast, you might want to take a stroll around the Lake Gardens, a lushly tropical area in the heart of Kuala Lumpur. Just walk and relax, umbrella-protected from the sun, preferably. Visit the Butterfly Farm or Bird Park you'll find there. Or find some shade near the football pitch and marvel at the lads who are running around kicking a ball and defying the searing heat.

Better than watching a nice lady iron your shirts.

Direct Marketing for a Mate
(Inspired by a True Story)

Are you tired to tears of being lonely?

Do you gaze at happy couples, walking hand-in-hand, with a sense of frustrated longing?

Are you, in the immortal words of The Spice Girls, living "forever, for the moment, for the ONE"?

Do you have something to sell, but no one really special to sell it to?

Try Direct Marketing.

Anyone who yearns for attention, and ultimately, someone to accept an offer and maintain a happily-ever-after relationship, could use a little help from Direct Marketing. Take your sorry, solitary self, for example.

What have you done so far? Roam the pubs trying to catch a desirable stranger's eye? Mingle amongst the masses with every other lonely heart - hoping against all hope to stand out in the crowd?

Hey, it's an approach most make, with some degree of occasional success. It's called, "getting lucky." Getting lucky is OK. I'd venture to guess that most of you would rather get lucky with the right person. Or at least, get lucky more often.

So here's what you do. A step-by-step guide for applying the Principles of Direct Marketing to your quest for a perfect mate ...

Your "Direct Marketing for a Mate" User's Guide

Step One: Cast a Net

You can do this a number of ways. Get hold of a list of people who are most likely to be receptive to what you have to offer. You could try one of those "Need a Friend?" services in the local classifieds.

Or if you're stranger-shy (or figure those services are littered with losers) try building your own prospect list. Every time you have an opportunity for contact, be sure to get at least a name, address and phone number. Business cards help. Little sheets of paper work fine, too.

But when you get the contact information, try also to jot down a few particulars. Whatever particulars are important to you ... the physical stuff like colour of eyes, height, vital stats ... or "inner soul" stuff like style and personality, hobbies, habits. If any of the above particulars annoys you (e.g., a habit of picking one's nose in public) feel free to crumple up the card or note and toss it in the nearest bin at your earliest convenience.

Step Two: Assign Values

After you've cast your net and collected enough desirable prospects, lay out all the bits of information on your dining room table. Look through your names, one by one, and create a ranking system. You can be as simple or as detailed as you want at this point, with high-to-low value categories, or subcategories within categories.

For example, a "5" could be assigned to all "Contact Them NOW" prospects. A "1" to "Contact them in a few months" hopefuls. A "5A" to "Perfect, Likes to Dance". A "5D" to "Perfect, but Dances Like a Zombie". You get the idea, yes?

If you're really cool, load all this in your hand phone so you can just speed-dial at the push of a button.

Step Three: Make Contact

Try your high-value prospects first. But take note: Just because they're on your list, it doesn't mean they're pre-sold. You still have to package yourself. Do it honestly, though, because the good ones can smell a phony a mile away. It is important to look good, to sound right, to communicate with a pleasingly personable tone and manner. But what you have to say is much more important than how you say it.

And you can substantially increase your chances for success with an offer they can't refuse. A romantic dinner-for-two is a traditional favourite, but it really depends on who you're talking to. One man's dinner-for-two is another man's jogging-together-around-the-Lake Gardens. Just make sure your offer fits you, your target, and your objectives.

Step Four: Never Say Goodbye

OK, so they had other commitments on your first try. If they didn't say, "Get Lost, Loser" try again in the near future. Just because they didn't jump at the first chance doesn't mean they're not dating, or not interested. Keep at it, at least until you're darn sure they don't want you.

Step Five: Keep Mining

Once you've gone through all the time and trouble of collecting contact information, keep your data fresh. People move. Change jobs. Get married. You must keep active if only to keep your information up-to-date. Active "mining" of your data is also important if you want a truly long-lasting relationship, because building a good relationship takes time.

Step Six: Track Results

You can learn a lot from your successes and your failures. Keep doing what works for you, and avoid the things you know you've done wrong.

Now ... stop feeling sorry for yourself and go out and get your perfect mate. Just add a little Direct Marketing method to your madness, and everything will work out just fine.

"Wah, so much. Very Expensive!"

How much is too much to spend on creating communications for your brand? That is, communications for the purpose of sales?

Your answer should NOT be: "Anything more than what I'm spending now."

Any amount you spend on brand communications ought to be linked to what can be achieved in sales. Advertising budgets are the spawn of previous profits, and married to all the marketing elements that make potential profits likely. You have to be open to the idea that, given a sensible rationale, what you are spending now may well be less than it should be.

A "sensible rationale" is infinitely easier to form when you are considering the tactics of direct response marketing. Direct response, of course, means the measure of consumer activity specifically connected to your communications. This measurability ultimately allows a precise calculation of the return on your investment as related to sales conversions.

And along the way, you also discover very useful information about consumer interest - or disinterest - in your selling message and communication technique.

If you are considering an email campaign, for example, you will have many opportunities to measure the return on your communication investment. From open rates, click-through and opt-out rates to website interaction, forwarded email rates and subsequent online sales.

Direct Response press or broadcast also can be tracked from ad burst to conversions, as consumers begin to call in or request information and those individuals are successfully sold.

So let me ask my opening question slightly differently: If I could show you the amount of sales you would need to pay for your brand promotion, would you at least consider my proposed cost for the communication?

Your answer should NOT be: "If you could guarantee you'll achieve the amount of sales I'll need, sure."

Direct Marketers are, alas, not God. Godlike, to be sure, but not God. Please remember the "death and taxes" rule. And also consider that unless the selling process is a simple two-step, e.g., 1) Respond and 2) Pay, like a Home Shopping Network scenario, there will be a conversion stage. At that stage it will likely be your agents or sales people doing the selling. Totally out of a Direct Marketer's immediate control, and in the hands of a higher power.

So let's get back to reality. You want a direct response press ad. Your product is a club membership with an average cost of RM1000. (Give me a break here ... the math will be easier.)

I've just shown you a brilliant ad that prominently displays a toll-free number directly inbound to your sales agents. My job is to get people to call that number; your job is to get them to pay for a membership then and there. Or at least capture contact data for mail or in-person follow-up. And then get them to pay.

The first step is to calculate the allowable promotional cost for each new membership, based on your desired profit:

Selling Price: RM1000. Less Your Costs (Costs of Goods; what you spend internally to achieve each membership, like salaries): RM300. That means each new membership sold contributes RM700 (Selling Price - Costs) to what's required to break-even on your promotional costs.

But, of course, you want to see some profit. Let's say you desire a RM600 profit on each membership. That means your allowable promotional cost per membership is RM100 (Contribution to Breakeven - Desired Profit).

So you now have a per-sale promotional cost limit that will give you a profit of RM600 on each membership. Now, let's get to your budget. I have miraculously created a powerful, responsive ad for the measly total sum of RM10,000. The cost of a single, 1/2-page, F/C insertion is RM29,000. Total promotion cost: RM39,000.

How many sales are required to cover the promotion cost of RM39,000? Just divide Total Promotion Cost by Allowable Cost Per Order: RM39,000 / 100 = 390. You would need 390 new memberships to pay for your promotion cost, at a desired profit of RM600 per membership.

What kind of conversion rate, calls turned into sales, would you need to get 390 new memberships? The newspaper's circulation is 140,000. 390 / 140,000 x 100 = .28%. (That's POINT-Two-Eight percent, in case you missed the decimal mark.) Just .28% - 390 of the newspaper's total readers - would have to call and purchase a membership to cover the cost of your promotion.

One step further. Not everyone who calls will become a member. But by now, you should know your average conversion rate of prospects to customers. Is it, say, 25%? If your sales agents close, on average, 25% of the time, you would need to get at least 1,560 calls to achieve 390 new memberships. If your closing rate is better than that - and remember, these people are calling you, interested and pre-disposed to a sale - you'll need fewer total calls. That's where God comes in again.

As for the ability of the ad to elicit response, even just 1,560 calls, you must employ Direct Marketing experts. There are many creative techniques that work together to maximize results, and only the experts know them all.

"Only RM10,000 for a direct response press ad? Wah, so cheap!"

Is America Getting Dumber
... and Is It Contagious?

Long before Al Gore, the former next President of the United States, invented the Internet, the late, great David Ogilvy had some advice for marketers of his time.

The thoroughly knowledgeable man, backed by facts, no doubt, (he was into statistical research even before he became a creative guru) wrote: The consumer is not a moron; she's your wife."

That was then. But what if the "intelligence factor" is different now. What if consumers are becoming more "duh"?

Think about that. If consumers are actually getting dumber, some marketers would find reason to rejoice. Assuming dumber consumers have money to spend, their diminished level of smarts would be a boon to anyone marketing unnecessary, unwanted, sub-quality goods. All it would take would be an appeal to dumbed-down desires, tapped or implanted. Right?

On the other hand, marketers of goods or services that require some degree of consumer thought, say complicated propositions, or anything that really required a feature-benefit extraction the intellectually challenged might not easily comprehend, well, time to sob. Or is it?

It seems there is a flurry of books being published in the U.S. that claim not only are Americans becoming dumber, they are also arrogantly "hostile to knowledge".

This may not come as a surprise to many of you. After all, Americans are the populous who elected George W. Bush ... not once, but TWICE. Not exactly an argument for the collective intelligence of my fellow citizens.

In an article in The Washington Post by author Susan Jacoby (*The Age of American Unreason*), the causes-and-effects for Americans becoming a "nation of dunces" are a triangulation of three connected vectors. One is a stunning decline in reading, a triumph of video - including all its digital forms - over print. The result has been a withering of our ability to concentrate and a decline of absorbed detail.

The second vector, Ms. Jacoby claims, is "the erosion of general knowledge". As focus and detail are sacrificed to visual hedonism, we become increasingly less informed. But Ms. Jacoby's third vector is the real stunner. Not only are Americans increasingly less focused and informed, they are becoming "arrogant about that lack of knowledge".

She writes: "The problem is not just the things we do not know (consider the one in five American adults who, according to the National Science Foundation, thinks the sun revolves around the Earth); it's the alarming number of Americans who have smugly concluded that they do not need to know such things in the first place."

Yikes. Does this "anti-rationalism" mean that selling to Americans no longer requires a logical, linear, persuasive argument? Is there no further need for a uniquely positioned product or service, given the presumption that the American consumer won't "get it" and probably doesn't care anyway?

And is "anti-rationalism" a cultural cancer created by a combination of factors that exist only in America? In a New York Times interview, Ms. Jacoby said that's a discussion she would welcome. Why does America seem especially vulnerable, she ponders, considering similar "infotainment" distractions around the globe?

Keep in mind that a purchase decision requires a financial sacrifice. A consumer has to be willing to part with cash, and that means there must be answers to the question: "Is this thing worth it?" But the problem in America, which I believe could easily extend beyond its borders, is monopolizing a consumer's attention in the first place.

This, of course, is not a new marketing challenge. But if today's consumers are becoming even more disassociated and, in fact, disdainful of knowledge, individualized, one-on-one communications will become an increasingly important part of a marketer's arsenal.

Targeting will increase the chance of refocusing their attention. Personalised messages, addressing specific needs and wants, would help maintain their interest. The opportunity for immediate response will help keep the length of the selling process to a minimum.

Direct Marketing has always been a smart seller's weapon of choice. But in a world of chronically distracted, "I couldn't care less" consumers, it could quite possibly be the only weapon that would work.

Bringing in the Bucks:
The Art of Fundraising

I was tickled pink to hear that PT Foundation won the first Malaysian NGO of the Year Award.

This inaugural moment happened on 19 May, 2008. Hosted by The Resource Alliance, supported by ExxonMobil Exploration & Production Inc, organized by The International Resource (Asia) in association with Nanyang Foundation, China Press, Life Publishers and Star Foundation, winning the top award is meaningful in many ways.

First, and perhaps most of all, it marks at least two unique milestones in charitable efforts here in Malaysia. The first: PTF was initially known as the Pink Triangle. A couple of years before I came to live and work in Malaysia in 1989, a couple of guys became acutely aware that their friends were becoming sick. And the prognosis was death.

These young and aware Malaysian men began to fight back. Or at least do something. They began with telephone counseling about HIV/AIDS and sexuality. More about what they now do later.

Keep in mind the mind of the times. In the U.S., the impending epidemic (now a pandemic) was evident. President Ronald Reagan was informed, but then it was considered a "gay disease" and that particular cowboy decided to look the other way.

Think of that for a moment. If the American president at the time had realized a true worldwide danger (talk about Weapons of Mass Destruction) funds could have been commanded by the world's superpower to pour into research that just might have prevented a global spread before the damn thing began to mutate.

And think of the immense daring it took for the founders of Pink Triangle, one of whom in its core group was Raymond Tai, the current Acting Executive Director & Programme Director, to take even one step in the direction of comforting a seriously disenfranchised community in Malaysia. In 1987.

Yes, the "positioning" of Pink Triangle, for all concerned, was a bit different then. It was at the time, more publicly about drug users. But still, they directly served a gay community. It was a Malaysian commonwealth that was becoming ill, and without doubt, they informed that community well enough to prevent the situation as it is today from becoming even worse.

You want the stats? Well, here they are anyway. As of this writing, 42 million people worldwide are living with HIV/AIDS. Including the growing number of HIV positive Malaysians. Statistics show at least 16 persons nationwide are reported HIV positive every single day here in Malaysia. In Malaysia's MSM community - Men who have Sex with Men - 10% of those who are tested by the Free Anonymous HIV screenings provided by PT Foundation are HIV positive. 28 million have died from this pandemic.

So that covers the Malaysian milestone. A non-profit organization, now dedicated to "providing HIV/AIDS education, prevention, care and support programmes, sexuality awareness and empowerment programmes for vulnerable communities in Malaysia" (quote from PTF's website), wins the first of an annually planned Best Malaysian NGO award. Awesome.

The second thing that is appreciably notable about this award is that PTF must be doing a lot of things right. The award is based on how well the NGO is governed, how transparent it is, with clear and reliable reports and communications, how they safeguard financial resources ... and how effective and strategic are their fundraising abilities.

To that last criterion, I answer all who are know wondering, "What the hell does any of this have to do with Direct Marketing?"

Seriously, I have absolutely no knowledge of what PT Foundation is currently doing in terms of fundraising. But my guess is, with this prized affirmation, they are doing it right.

And that would be a combination and culmination of the following "to do" list for any organization that might ask for a charitable contribution.

One of the first things to do is to develop a fundraiser's equivalent of advertising's Unique Selling Proposition - USP. This helps to settle your organization's identity differently than the huge number of others who are also asking for contributions. Acclaimed "relationship fundraising" expert Ken Burnett called this statement a UGP - or Unique Giving Proposition.

Next is targeting. Examine the potential of corporations and individuals who are the most likely to respond to your particular cause. This is not an easy thing to do, given the mission of an organization like PTF, and huge assumptions I'm certain must be made. But without a sense of who you think will give the most, nothing can be planned - associations, alliances, mailing lists, email, media - nothing. So it must be done.

There is so much more. Pricing considerations. Do you want annual commitments? Monthly? How often and how much do you tap your current donors? And how? One annual event or many? How do you compete with other fundraising activities? And how can you, if it is indeed possible, reciprocate with other charities and share donor lists?

I have expressed my amazement (and delight) at how Borack Obama smashed records for online donations during his presidental primary campaign (see page 62). Yes, it's politics, and that makes it different. And yet, his DM/CRM online guys have done what many others might copy, a blueprint for money-raising success. Here's my hero's list of money- and activism-related activities that could inspire a long-term connection with any cause:

- Online Blog. Your chance to catch up on latest news, photos and videos related to your organization
- Issues. Also online. What issues affect your target's desire to get involved?
- Organizing. How to connect with other supporters in your area?
- Spread the Word. An easy way to introduce your friends and family to the cause.
- My Favorite: An online calling tool that gives you and only you, people to call to enlist their support.
- Plus ... Merchandising. Never forget the power of a t-shirt. Or coffee mug.

Anyway. Congrats to PT Foundation. And all the best for fundraisers deserving of future rewards. Got a good cause? Bring in the bucks. Sensibly and strategically.

CRM ... Magic Letters?

"In-the-know" marketers here and around the world are frequently uttering a sequence of three consonants: C-R-M. In that order.

These letters, when spoken before current or would-be clients, are meant to mesmerize. They are intended to elevate the listener to a nirvana of marketing investment returns that were simply unimaginable ... until now.

Repeat after me ... C-R-M. They are almost always spoken as if "C-R-M" is a mantra that has suddenly appeared before us like a celestial beacon. A shiny, new epiphany brought to you by the Gods of Sales and Profits.

Guess what. CRM is nothing new.

CRM has always been a tool of the Direct Marketing trade. Direct Marketing helps you find customers. Then it helps you keep them and make them more valuable to you. That's CRM. Plain and simple.

Tech-wizards and jargon groupies have latched on to these three little letters like a flea to my neurotic dog Lori (see page 19). They suck the lifeblood out of the true purpose and meaning of CRM by reverently introducing this long-term strategy as the latest miracle cure for any number of marketing ills.

Well, it is and it isn't. You can and should employ a CRM strategy, because when you do (and do it right), you will significantly increase your profitability. But success requires an unwavering commitment. Now and forever. And you must instill a customer-oriented mindset that is consistently apparent through all organizational levels of your company - from CEO to front-liners to delivery personnel.

Not easy, but not impossible. No company does it perfectly. A few get it right more often that not. And most, well, they don't have a clue.

Take Cannot-Be-Named Airlines, for example. A true story. Wish I could identify the perp.

A few years ago, I flew back to the U.S. on holiday with two Malaysian friends and their 13-month old baby. On Cannot-Be-Named (CBN) Airlines. Now, it's never easy travelling for 22 hours in a steel pod, and even more difficult with an infant who is experiencing her very first transoceanic flight. CBN didn't make it any easier.

The journey began well. From KL to Japan, the crew delivered the baby's meal in a plastic bag. An assortment of three little jars, one of which was a reddish-brown mash labeled "Lasagna with Meat Sauce". Something only a baby could love. But not if it's served freezer-cold. And it was.

So my friend asked a flight attendant if she would warm the thing up. She said, "Sure!" with a smile so broad it lit up the plane's entire cattle-section. The attendant even offered a couple of serving options: "In the jar, or would you like it in a little bowl?"

So far, so good. But the journey from Japan to the U.S. was another matter altogether.

A fresh crew was brought it for this leg, and each and every one of them was the body and personality type we frequent CBN fliers have come to know so well. Former high-security prison guards who have quelled one-too-many escape attempts. Big breasted and matronly. And the women were, too.

Again, when the baby's first meal arrived, it was served cold. Chilled liver and onions anyone? No thank you. Again, the request to heat the thing up. Her reply was equal to the temperature of the baby jar in discussion. No way. You take it like you get it. Apparently, what's possible in one Boeing is not possible in another.

More incidents followed. Time for the adults' meal. Mom, with baby in arms. Father asking: "Could you save one tray? That way, I can eat first, then hold the baby later while mom eats." In a tone that would make Hitler proud, the attendant replied: "No. You take your trays now. I can't guarantee you'll have a tray later." She then sandwiched both trays and plopped them on his armchair table. She neglected to ask, "Chicken or Beef?"

Sometime later, somewhere over the Pacific, the baby was resting comfortably at mom and dad's feet. Now, this is not allowed, and both mom and dad knew it. Just a little illicit break from hours of arm-cradling.

An attendant here-to-fore unseen (where do they all hide?) barreled up the aisle and spotted the indiscretion. She said, "You can't ..." then stopped in mid-sentence. Dad was about to apologize when she stormed off to fetch the Japanese interpreter.

This CBN flight attendant, who happened to be African American (see relevance below), instantly assumed that because my friend was "Oriental" he 1) was Japanese and 2) couldn't speak English. What, she couldn't just talk to him herself, first? As an African American, isn't she at least a tiny bit familiar with racial prejudice? My friend is one of the most English-articulate people I know. And Chinese, thank you very much. He was not amused.

After our arrival in the U.S., and following a few nasty days of jet-lag recovery, my friend decided to email the Chief Executive Officer of CBN Airlines via online customer service at their website. An automated reply came back stating that while personal replies normally take 3-4 days, please expect a reply within 7-10 while the system is being upgraded. 7-10 days later, no reply. 3 weeks. No reply. No reply at all to date.

Hullo? Anybody home? 10 strikes and you're out. My friend, and his wife, and, I presume, the baby as well, have vowed never to fly the unfriendly CBN Airlines skies again. Trust me. They won't.

Are CBN flight attendants part of an airline's CRM programme? Yes. An integral part. The customer service facility at a website? Of course. The person who is supposed to provide a personal email reply? Absolutely. The CEO? Yes again, assuming they have one. There's been no proof of his or her existence thus far.

How about systems and software? If you have that in place, as CBN Airlines certainly does, do you have a CRM programme? Obviously not, citing CBN as a prime example. Technology is a data management and delivery device and nothing more.

The only "magic" words that will make your CRM programme work are these: Sincere Human Care. But like anything magical, you must truly believe to make it real.

Welcome to the Neighborhood

The "Tree House", as I called it, was my first home in Malaysia.

It's a huge bungalow, nestled at the base of an expansively forested hilly area called Bukit Gasing, or Gasing Heights.

The only thing behind this wooden structure is thick, tropical jungle as far as you can see. And the house is perched just high enough to have a view of the neighborhood in front, an old suburban area adjacent to Kuala Lumpur.

As you walk up to the house, there's a lawn on your left, about 30 yards wide at the low area, tapering upwards about 40 yards, forming a green equivalent to a gigantic piece of pie. At the long outer edge of the lawn, more jungle.

The house itself is made entirely of wood, including the floors, with tiled exceptions in the kitchen and bathrooms. Hence, "The Treehouse". You get from the carport to the living room area with a short climb up a flight of stairs.

A quick turn to your right at the top brings you to a vast living room area. Shuttered floor-to-ceiling windowed doors open up the entire front of the house to a narrow outside balcony with neighborhood view. More shutter windows open up on the side for lawn and jungle view.

What a great party place that was. And a terrific perch to experience the "other" wildlife. Parrots. Gibbons. Monster lizards. A python I suspect ate my cat. Monkeys invaded the place once, nearly giving my housekeeper a heart attack. She turned up a tape she was playing (remember cassettes?) to get rid of them.

I live in a less eventful area now. But I still get monkeys.

Buying and Selling in Bliss
... with Extra Cheese

In a perfect marketing world, you would know who is buying your product, when they buy, where they buy, how much they buy, how often and by what means ... customer by customer.

In that perfect world, you would also know who does not buy your brand and why they don't. You would know if they buy a competitive brand and why ... and when, where, how much, how often and by what means. Prospect by prospect.

Although a "perfect marketing world" may be currently unrealistic, you can at least, take "one step closer" to it, as my colleague Drayton Bird suggests. So what if you do? Would the grey haze of imperfection dissipate so sunlit rays of blissful happiness can shine down on the earth's capitalists and consumers alike?

Well, yeah. Or at least the bliss would begin. Take just one step towards that perfect world - through Direct Marketing - and you could make quite a bit of that annoying haze go away right now.

Identified Customers

Do you have individual buying profiles for each and every one of your customers? If they are buying from you directly, you should. If you don't, you're missing an ocean of marketing opportunities.

It's easy to gather and take advantage of buying profiles. Just record and store consumer activity on an individual level. Make sure you have the information you need for a meaningful marketing analysis across your entire customer base. And be sure you can select and group criteria that could be used to create a communications strategy.

Take Cannot-Be-Named (CBN) Pizza, for example. I'm sure they know how many pizzas I've ordered from them since they established here in Malaysia. They should have the orders by date. If they wanted to, they could probably see a pattern in my pizza preference.

What could they do, marketing-wise, that would make me happy ... and increase their sales?

First they could calculate my value to them. Let's say they did that, and discovered that compared to others in their customer base, I'm pretty high value but could probably order from them more often. In other words, high value (based on past orders) but not enough loyalty (because other high value customers order more often). In fact, I do give The Other Guys a call now and then.

Once they've calculated my value, CBN could do a number of things to discourage any future calls to The Other Guys.

Let's say they are about to promote a brand new pizza choice or introduce a special offer. They could contact to me (and others like me) directly - ahead of any advertising or leaflet housedrops - and identify me as a special customer. Advance notice of the upcoming deal would make me feel that I'm important to them. An exclusive coupon with a valued customers-only offer would make me smile ... and order.

If CBN examined their database, they would discover that 90% of my many delivery orders have been for thin crust pepperoni, regular with extra cheese. How about a "Here's a Special Deal on Your Favourite Pizza!" communication? All high-value customers with a high percentage of repeat orders in their pizza-consuming histories would receive it. CBN could personalise each individual's "favourite" pizza on the coupon.

Expensive? Well, not cheap. But figure the promotion cost against the potential return on investment. These are high-value customers and very likely responders. You'd probably need to mail or email to a moderately large base to economically justify this type of personalised promotion. But don't forget to calculate the long-term value of these customers. If it all equates to a promotion that adds profit short-term and keeps valued customers longer, then it's a no-brainer.

Non-Identified Customers & Prospects

If you don't sell to customers in a way that enables an immediate database, don't despair. There are many ways to identify buyers of your brand, and build the marketing information you require for future communications and on-going selling opportunites. Name-and-contact-gathering on-pack promotions, contests, purchase-connected take-ones ... these are just a few ways to add these customers to your database.

The most important thing to know about any one who is not buying your brand is if he or she would *ever* buy your brand. And the easiest and most reliable way to obtain that bit of knowledge is to ask them to "raise their hands." At the very least, you ask, "Interested?" If they answer "Yes!", and your question has been formed to avoid a flippant response, you've identified a potential buyer.

Where can you ask prospects to "raise their hands" in interest? Responsive advertising (print or broadcast) events and exhibitions plus telemarketing, websites, mobile phones, social networks. Again, the list goes on.

And as I mentioned earlier, while "perfect marketing" may not be currently attainable, interactive media and technology make it increasingly possible. But perfect marketing, if it is ever to occur, will always depend on your knowledge of customers and prospects, and how well you use it.

Don't Bark Up the Wrong Loyalty Tree

The only living things in this world that are loyal without effort are dogs. Even then, you must feed them regularly, and treat them with a measure of kindness.

Some dogs are more tolerant of neglect than others. But more often than not, if you lay down a bowl of canned mystery meat on a daily basis, they will love you like you're god.

Note to loyalty marketers: Your customers are not dogs. Laying down a regular bowl of tidbits is not nearly enough to keep customers loyal.

Most loyalty "schemes" in this market involve a card, points and reward redemption. This may be a good start for some business categories, enough for a few, but dangerously inadequate for many. When you judge the value of any loyalty scheme, you need to take a long, hard look at your customer profile, and the long-term value of their loyalty.

Even loyal customers, the ones who choose your brand consistently, may often dabble. Why? A price promotion perhaps. Or special offer. Many brands have a generic value. And even when there are clear brand advantages, customers don't see the totality of value on a daily basis. Brand value is engendered over a long period of time, and only then, if an effort has been made to confirm the brand's undeniable role in the lives of each and every customer.

To identify value that would appeal to your customers, you must determine what they need and want. Everyone wants to pay less and get more. But what else? What value can you add to your brand? It doesn't have to cost you money in discounts, and probably shouldn't. Discounts regularly attract the customers you already have - who would happily pay you the normal price anyway.

If you're managing a loyalty scheme for petrol, for example, you might logically assume that partnerships with driving/car-related marketers would add value to your brand. That would certainly be a safe assumption in the Malaysian market, where loyalty schemes are becoming increasingly identical.

Banks might also safely assume that credit card customers might naturally appreciate sound financial advice (your products) in addition to the accustomed rewards. Your assumption becomes more valid if you segment your database to identify particularly attractive spenders and payers.

But while logic and experience may help identify needs and wants, don't rely solely on assumptions. Research it by auditing your customer database. In fact, asking for someone's opinion is an effective way to strengthen loyalty. It's also an easy and relatively inexpensive task that pays off in valuable information.

Whatever you spend on loyalty should be in direct proportion to both immediate returns and the long-term value of your customers. Yes, it's important to make a sale, here and now. It's also vitally important to encourage - and realize - future sales. When you rationalize your loyalty marketing investment you have to factor in both, or any scheme becomes financially indefensible.

Justifying your investment in loyalty, however, is far easier than maintaining a programme that is lovingly devoted to customers. So while you're keeping a watchful eye on your bottom line, make the care and nurture of customers a top priority. Serve them more than mere tidbits.

Then and Now

Blink.

And it's 20 years later. Still in Kuala Lumpur, Malaysia.

There are a gazillion more cars on the road. Most seem steered by drivers who believe they have a license to kill.

But there are also more roads. Now you just take aim at your destination and choose a network of links, highways and super highways, and pay the obligatory tolls. It takes less than 4 hours to travel from Kuala Lumpur all the way north to Penang Island. It used to take well over 7.

And what a hellish trip that was. The two-lane road traversed through every tiny kampung (village) on Malaysia's western coastline. Get stuck behind a slow moving lorry (inevitable and often) and you had a choice. Follow patiently or risk the Malaysian Death Pass, a maneuver that would always end within inches of oncoming vehicles. If you were lucky.

Back in my early days in KL, there was a single, solitary nightclub. One. It was called The Tin Mine, an odd combination of dancing and backgammon.

I once played a few games with a local stranger in the din of the Tin and soundly thrashed the fella. He was not amused. After, another stranger took me aside and asked "Do you know who you just whipped?" I didn't. "That's Gaffar Baba's son!" he exclaimed, all wild-eyed and goofy. Apparently I had risked the wrath of the Deputy Prime Minister's progeny. (Gaffar Baba is now deceased.)

Choices for western food then were slim. Now there are literally hundreds. Most tourists automatically make a stop at The Hard Rock Café, which had me on its barstools from its beginning on November 23, 1991.

Funny. I always seem to end up talking about food and drink. Cheers!

Lessons from a Car Mechanic

On a jaunt to Desa Sri Hartamas, a treandy and porpular K.L. "suburb", I discovered two wonderful things.

The first discovery: a quiet, English-style pub with a decent happy hour and absolutely fabulous food. And the second: a couple of shoplots down, a very busy car repair shop.

The owner of the pub is a delightful retired Brit, as quiet and unassuming as the golden oldies that play in the background. The owner of the car repair shop is a youngster (by Crocker-years) who is in constant movement, a kid of ceaseless energy and verve.

I was introduced to the car repair guy over a few frosty mugs with a couple of friends. We talked about his business, which by the numbers of cars rolling in and out of his shop, was constantly brisk. He's obviously doing well, and I wondered out loud about his secrets for success.

As it turns out, this budding entrepreneur has the beginnings of a very promising Customer Relations Management programme. Add a little IT, and he could put the big boys to shame.

Lesson Number One

While my new mechanic friend fully believes in his skills, and ultimately, his delivered product, he understands there are a lot of other talented mechanics out there. Here's a lesson for managers of even the strongest brands - you're not as strong as you may think you are. It's far better to be less confident about your brand equity, and downright deadly to be cocky.

These days, while brand-building is a fundamental marketing activity and ought to be an on-going goal, thinking above and beyond the basics is essential.

Lesson Number Two

The car kid has also formulated a solid business philosophy: A Fair Price for Honest Service. Now, you may think that sounds simplistic. Maybe so, but he believes in it, and delivers it. And he fully understands why he must. I've seen countless plaques hung in various corporate reception areas that express similar intentions. But more often than not, there is little evidence of them on the front-lines.

You may also think that a business belief such as his is much easier to deliver on a small scale. Nonsense. Even if you're a huge conglomerate, you ought to have an internal communication programme that reminds and instructs and emblazons the soul of your corporate philosophy into the mindset of your entire working staff. This is especially important for the people who confront customers face-to-face, but equally vital for anyone responsible for the quality and delivery of your product or service.

Lesson Number Three

The car kid knows repair competition is fierce. Let's face it, competition is fierce in any business category. Consumers have tons of choices, and they do choose and switch, even if they're brand-loyal. They may switch temporarily during a promotion or because of a cost-cut. But they will switch forever if they perceive a particular brand offers added value in the long-term.

So he's added a 24-hour breakdown service. Just one call, anytime, and he'll get a mechanic to your car, repair if he can and tow if he must. A lot of the big guys do that. But few of the small shops do. With one line on his business card that offers the promise of added service, he has set himself far above and beyond many of his competitors.

Lesson Number Four

As we were sitting and chatting at the pub, just two doors down from his repair shop, I became aware of another of the car kid's business assets. Quite a few people work in that area, and he knew a great many of them. When they walked by on their way to their transport and the comforts of home, there was always a mutually friendly greeting, and an occasional short conversation.

A business asset? Yes, and probably one of the most important he could ever have. It would be less important if he had developed this network of prospects with the intention of improving profits. But he believes that the natural order of life, in business or otherwise, is to be nice to people. If he didn't truly believe that, there would be far fewer greetings and friendly conversations. And there would be far fewer "friends" who would take their cars to his shop for servicing.

The lesson here is that it's not enough to promote "friendly service". In fact, it's far more important to create friendships, for the sole purpose of a personal relationship. With those altruistic intentions, the business will come.

Lesson Number Five

I asked if he had a computer in his shop. Nope. I suggested that he think about that relatively inexpensive investment, along with the addition of a simple database solution. He could keep track of who came in for what, and send out little reminders of regular service intervals, or promote a special offer.

He liked the idea. Another channel for delivering service. The lesson: Always be on the lookout for new and improved ways to satisfy your customers' needs and wants.

Love of Money & The Root
of All Retail Marketing Evil

A show of hands, please.

Who wants to get filthy, stinking, the-sky-is-the-limit rich?

You're in the retail business. You sell stuff. Another show of hands, please. Who would like to sell so much stuff that you actually go deaf from the constant ringing of cash registers?

Who doesn't want to get wallet-bulging rich? Oh sure, there have been some among us who'd rather live the Walden's Pond, simpler-is-better life. Frankly, I believe those people are nuts.

SHOW ME THE MONEY!

Yeah, but there's a flaw in that particular movie sound-bite. Jerry Maguire suddenly turned his back on the cold promotion of corporate athletic endorsements and became a caring idealist. Yet his single remaining client still insisted ... SHOW ME THE MONEY. He wanted to get rich, just like the rest of us greedy realists.

The flaw is this: Where does the money come from? Does it come from your sheer determination? Your talents? Your winning smile?

No. In the case of professional football, it comes from the fans. The good folks who watch the game, and ultimately buy products attached to the image of your performance.

In the case of you hard-working, inventory-calculating retailers, the money you make comes from your customers. It such a simple reality. Cash doesn't just magically appear. It is delivered to you by humanoids. Why is that so tough to remember?

The purpose of a retail business, like any business, is not to make profits. You have to earn returns on your investments, of course, but you will ultimately fail if you're only thinking about those ringing cash registers. You must go beyond SHOW ME THE MONEY and concentrate more on making and keeping customers ... profitably.

I've related - many times - the story of this filthy rich businessman from Texas. A reporter asked: "How do you make your millions?" He said, in that rather annoying George W. Bush Texas drawl, "Why it's simple son. I find out what my customers need and want, I give it to them, and I get rich."

Another filthy rich used car salesman from America (thankfully not a Texan) said this: "My next customer comes from my first sale." This is not a very Asian way of thinking. Here we happily grab the money and hope for the appearance of another customer.

Open your doors and they will come? Not these days. You ain't the only retailer in town. Consumers have endless choices. Down the street, or off in cyberspace. The days of a retailer's control of current and prospective customers are long gone.

Unless ... you find out what your customers need and want, and give it to them. Only then will you have a chance to make and keep customers longer. Only then, will you be in a position to be profiled on "Lifestyles of the Rich and Famous."

Yes, you still have to acquire new customers. But remember this always: Acquiring a new customer costs 5 to 10 times as much as retaining an existing customer.

And hear this from research analyst Alex Brown: "U.S. organisations lose one-half of their customers every five years. A 5% incremental improvement in the customer retention rate could have the effect of doubling profits." I repeat: Doubling Profits.

Enough preaching. I will assume you are converted. So how do you go about turning your new-found belief into action?

Here come the scary bits.

For starters ... you need a Central Marketing Database. Then ... you need a Customer Relationship Management Strategy (CRM). It's not quite as scary as it sounds. But if you have a large retail business with substantial volume, it's not a walk in the park either:

1) You will need to make an investment in technology - software and the people who run it.
2) You'll have to re-tool your marketing strategy into one that is technology-enabled.
3) Implementing a CRM Strategy will require operational changes in your organisation - including marketing, sales and service.
4) You will have to integrate all marketing communication contacts.
5) And importantly, you will need the ability to collect, manage and use information about your customers, effectively.

And everyone in your company - everyone - must be completely dedicated to making your CRM strategy work, long-term. Long-term, shared dedication at every level is critical, because if that is not the case, whatever you invest in technology will head south ... straight down the toilet. Along with your visions of a 6-month cross-company bonus, or any real opportunity to get filthy, stinking rich.

In other words, once you've got it, flaunt it. Often.

So let's take another leap and assume you have the framework in place to implement a CRM strategy. How do you make it work to your greatest advantage?

Gold-mining data. Here are 5 ideas that will help you increase your retail sales ... and some real-life examples. Not all the examples I'll show you are strictly retail, but the fundamental reasoning applies in every case.

1) Treat your most important customers differently.

Your Central Marketing Database should allow examination of each customer's worth. How much does she spend with you in a month or a year? How often does she make a purchase? In order to know this information, you need some device or method that can track individual sales - like an in-store credit card, or membership number scan.

A while back, DHL Malaysia introduced a new service called Asia Overnight. The mass of their customers received a flat direct mail package that explained the benefits of the service. Their high-value customers receive a different pack. A dimensional mailing that included a free, branded stop-watch that helped highlight the key benefit of guaranteed overnight delivery.

2) Offer off-site purchase and delivery by post

Convenience is king. That's why there are growing multitudes of people who are ordering products from websites. Security concerns have all but diminished.

But be forewarned. Research conducted by the Direct Marketing Association of America has indicated that more than a third of everyone who makes a website product purchase are disastified with what they receive and send it back. More than 40% say they would have liked to return the product but didn't want to endure the hassle or expense. Customer satisfaction is not being managed very well in cyberspace.

On the bright side, 20% say they are more likely to order from a website if there's a retail outlet nearby. Human contact still rules.

If you don't have a website, do mail-order catalogs. You can still identify branch outlets and encourage on-site purchases, but offer the convenience of mail-order delivery, too.

3) Identify prospects through an offer in your ads

Include a coupon for a purchase discount, but make sure it requires a name and contact information upon redemption. Or ask them to return a coupon to get your catalog - even if it's just a promotional catalog. Then get them on your database.

Seeing how many responses you get from offers in your ads can also help determine media effectiveness.

4) Ask smart questions

When you mail to your database to encourage a purchase, you also have the opportunity to ask simple questions. You can use the mailing to audit customer satisfaction, or ask about other products they might be interested in. You might also offer response options through questions, to determine the degree of purchase resistance to the product on-offer.

American Express mailed an upgrade promotion to their "green card" members. And they offered several response options. They wanted to know if the cardmembers were or would ever be interested in a Gold Card. And if they would someday want to upgrade, then when.

5) Use warranty cards to identify your customers

First, you have to make sure your warranty cards are marketing-friendly. Date and location of purchase, product code, name and address. If, for example, you identify a customer through a warranty card for a kitchen blender, you may consider them a prospect for other kitchen appliances in the future.

"Show Me How Much You Love Me!"

Retailers lament abysmal sales.

One-time dot-com zillionaires ponder their slide into financial oblivion.

Bankers reposition parity products to regain customers and fool nobody.

Brand leaders lose their crowns and wonder where and when the revolution started.

Well, boo hoo. Marketing ain't so simple anymore? Sure it is. We just have to remember our roots ... and then repot them.

What is it that will inspire someone to buy something these days? Well, you've got your same old benefits and features. You've got your competitive selling price. You've got your leadership position and bandwagon followers. And you've got that mystical "value of the brand."

But something has altered the relative importance of all the above factors. There is a new dynamic between choice and how choices are being made.

The bottom line is that consumers can get exactly what they want practically anywhere ... whether they find it housed in bricks and mortar or floating somewhere in cyberspace. And, man, are consumers getting fickle or what? Just ask those former dot-com zillionaires begging for spare change on the streets of Manhattan.

"Building the Brand" used to be, and still is I'd gather, the battle cry at my former agency. Here's the theory: The closer consumers become to all the real and apparent qualities of the brand, the more they are likely to choose that brand over others.

Every positive experience a consumer has with that brand is supposed to help cement the relationship. From the emotional invocations of packaging design through actual use or consumption.

So "The Brand", assuming the product or service it represents isn't crap, becomes an all-important reason for consumer choice. And the service experience - at the point of sale or after - is considered a "component" of the brand-building process.

Here's another theory, and one which I strongly advocate: Service is the thing now, even for brand believers. Consumers who have been buying the same brand for years want a more tangible decision-making ring to grasp. Why? Because they are not stupid. No matter how a "brand" has been positively impregnated, consumers know real value when they experience it. And they value service above all.

Remember the old axiom that's been hung on the walls of advertising agencies everywhere? "Clients will never care about how much you know until they know how much you care." From a consumer's perspective, let me rephrase that. "Customers will never care about your brand until you deliver customer care."

OK, it's not as neat and clever as the original. But you get the point, right? Establishing and maintaining brand values will always be vital. But more often than not, I reckon, brands will become established firmly and forever through the delivery of real service. And if you deliver service religiously and consistently over a long consumer-seller relationship ... you will rule. Richly.

In other words, anyone who sells anything ought to make service a number one priority. From the very moment a first purchase is made right through to a planned programme that puts service as the sole purpose for a seller's very existence. You must tell them you love them at every opportunity ... through direct communications that can range from a simple thank you to a series of added values that recognize their importance to you.

Some call it Customer Relationship Management (CRM). That's so cold and calculating. How about TLC (Tender Loving Care). For the consumer's benefit ... and yours.

D.M. the Beautiful

Realizing the Possibilities in America

Love her or scowl at her, there are many things America does right. Direct Marketing is one of them.

Here in Malaysia, we continue to merely dabble in D.M. The economic advantages of targeted communications have been pitched for yonks, with moderate success. Marketers are, however, finally starting to catch on to the benefits of nurturing relationships with their customers. But most are doing it poorly or without a comprehensive, long-term plan.

Some agencies have invested in D.M. training for their client service and creative staff. The problem with training is that you can teach the basics. You can define the discipline, offer a structure for a Direct Marketing brief, suggest a handy template for writing a letter. But you cannot teach a person to be passionate.

And passion is absolutely mandatory before anyone can even approach excellence. Quite a few of the "brand" advertisers possess passion. Few in Direct Marketing here do. And by passion I mean the unbridled joy that comes from analysing immediate results - good or bad ... the adrenaline-packed experience of devising a particularly clever targeted strategic approach ... heck, the unstoppable smile you get after writing a letter that positively soars with sell.

No, you cannot teach passion. But perhaps you can inspire it.

Which is why I began this chapter as a tribute to Direct Marketers in America. They have done some interesting work there, and maybe, by example, they may offer some source of inspiration to us here.

Burger Loyalty

Ah, those fast-food burger eaters are famously fickle. And promotion-sensitive. So how about a plan to keep them buying your brand long-term? Or at least beyond the usual short-term promotion period?

Some years ago, Burger King and eBay teamed up with a big idea, reportedly the first web-based loyalty programme in the fast-food business.

Buying certain food or drink items at Burger King restaurants around the U.S. earned points. These points could be deposited and tracked on the Burger King/eBay website. Participants could then use their points to bid on posted rewards.

Burger King offered 1 million rewards throughout 2002. (Hey, Burger King: How about relaunching the programme in Malaysia?)

Dynamic DRTV in 30 Seconds

Are we ready or not? DRTV can be much more than a distribution channel for selling non-stick frying pans and non-slip mats for your car's dash. America's National Football League (NFL) came up with another big idea that was bound to score.

The NFL Shop is the National Football League's direct marketing arm. They sell professional football merchandise like team-branded caps and tee-shirts. The NFL Shop got together with Reebok, who designed a special apparel line called NFL Gridiron Classics.

Thanksgiving Day in the U.S. is much more than stuffed turkey with all the trimmings. It is a very big day for American football. Here's what they planned:

During the game between the Detroit Lions and the Green Bay Packers, the coaches on both teams were to wear NFL Gridiron Classic apparel. In the first half, NFL Films would shoot footage of Lion's head coach Marty Mornhinweg in action as he goes about his business in a Gridiron Classics fleece. They would then package the footage into a 30-second DRTV spot to be shown in the second half. The spot would offer a toll-free number and its URL as an opportunity for consumers to request a catalog.

About 20 million Americans were expected to be watching the game. And while 30-second spots aren't usually effective for DRTV, NFL Shop's senior director of database marketing believed the event tie-in would make the spot perform. Wish I knew the results, but I predict he was right.

Righting a "Wrong"

Got a cause you really believe in? Why not make it the real thing, with a little help from direct electronic marketing?

That's what the folks at The Center for Science in the Public Interest (CSPI) did when Coca-Cola announced a marketing affiliation with the film *Harry Potter and the Sorcerer's Stone*. They felt that Coke was not healthy for children, and that the Harry Potter link-up would influence an unhealthy brand-choice.

So as Coca-Cola launched LiveTheMagic.com, a reading-promotion website the book's author J.K. Rowling made a pre-requisite if there was to be a product/film association, CSPI launched SaveHarry.com.

While LiveTheMagic.com allowed visitors to enter the "Search for the Sorcerer's Stone" Coca-Cola promotion, develop a list of books to fit their interest and create their own "storybook adventure", SaveHarry.com was a platform for protest.

The SaveHarry site included education about health issues associated with soft drinks, as well as a form letter email that refers to Coke as "liquid candy". More than 700,000 people visited the site by mid-November, a number bolstered by PR appearances by a CSPI spokesperson on national television.

In that same timeframe, 10,000 site visitors filled out and zapped the email form, which was automatically copied to CEOs of Warner Brothers, Scholastic, the U.S. publisher of Harry Potter books; and Bloomsbury Publishing Place, the U.K. publisher.

Several like-minded sites offered links to SaveHarry, and CSPI used all the emails to build a database for future causes.

Only in America? When you think about these and other innovative uses of Direct Marketing, think instead, "Why not Malaysia?"

Lessons from a Million Dollar Smile ...
Cavities and All

What have you ordered from a website lately?

Several years ago, my only purchases had been from Amazon ... a few books, some CD's and three DVD's. Then, during a holiday cocktail hour back home in America, my sister's neighbour told the story of Billy Bob teeth.

Invented by a D.D.S. and, at the time, available only on the internet, Billy Bob teeth came in a variety of hideously vulgar styles, and were designed to be custom-fitted by owners in the comfort of home. You just mix a little dental putty, apply to the Billy Bob teeth like denture adhesive, place over your own teeth, bite down and let it set for 10 minutes. Voila ... the world's ugliest smile, guaranteed to delight and nauseate simultaneously, over and over again.

Of course I had to check it out. So I rushed to the 'puter, searched for "Billy Bob Teeth" and there it was: www.billy-bob-teeth.com. One click brought me to a home page featuring the proud CEO modelling his flagship choppers. Also displayed in disturbingly lifelike colours, complete with gaps, plaque and bloody gums, were several other choices, including the new "Jethro" model, and "Deliverance" - a delightful tribute to in-breeding and white-water rafting trips gone wrong.

The site also include an "Owner's Manual" which was subtitled, "Everthin' yew needs to know when yew gots yer teeth in!" It suggested corny comments for various occasions, such as when you're stopped for speeding ("Gosh, officer. Do ya think ya cud give a poor ugly bastard a break?"), pick-up lines ("Yew know what they say 'bout the size of a man's teeth don'tcha?"), plus more bad humour than I care to repeat.

At just U.S.$10 a pop, I just couldn't resist. I imagined myself wearing them in oh-too-trendy Bangsar in Malaysia during a Friday night happy hour.

Just two days after I placed my order, I watched as the Tonight Show's Jay Leno teased Billy Bob Thorton about the website. The talented actor/director/writer shrugged the non-related product off with a chuckle ... as millions of viewers were exposed to what amounted to unpaid advertising for Billy Bob Teeth.

My not-so-shiny new teeth arrived within 10 days. The product delivered was exactly the product I anticipated. Expectations were well managed by Billy Bob.

Also included: A letter, congratulating me on my good sense and now-greatly-enhanced sexual prowess, written in the same dumb hillbilly tone. It also encouraged additional orders. To help me along toward that end, a catalog and order form. Oddly, the website address mentioned in the catalog - www.nastyteeth.com - was different than the one I had originally logged onto, but at least an online order alternative was also provided.

So what lessons can marketers take away from this e-commerce success story?

For starters, you can still get rich in cyberspace. The inventor and marketer of Billy Bob Teeth has undoubtedly hung up his drill in favour of holidays in the Bahamas because he followed a few simple rules:

- Create a strong product positioning and strengthen it throughout your site and in all promotional materials.
- Don't spend a zillion dollars on advertising if you can't possibly get a return on your investment quickly. Take advantage of PR and, if you'll excuse this coincidental pun, word-of-mouth.
- Don't take yourself too seriously. You don't have to resort to cornball humour, and certainly shouldn't with serious products and services. But no matter what you're selling, keep your messages human and conversational.
- Make sure that what appears and is described on your website is exactly what you'll be sending to your customers. Order satisfaction with e-commerce purchases is dismally low because what customers "see" is not what they end up getting.
- Don't just fill orders ... encourage additional sales with each delivery. And don't rely solely on returns to your website. Offer options for snail-mail orders as well ... and include a letter and brochure or catalog.
- Delivery no later than 10 to 14 days after an order. Delays will kill any prospective future orders.

If you've guessed that the above tips are fundamental rules of Direct Marketing - applied to cyberspace - you've guessed correctly. If you think you can ignore these basics and still be a successful e-commerce entrepreneur, think again. Selling stuff direct-to-consumers requires the principles of DM in any medium, including the web.

SPAM: The Good and the Ugly

SPAM, the Good.

SPAM is an international star. Created by the Hormel company in Austin, Minnesota ahead of World War II, the easily-transportable canned luncheon meat was a G.I. staple.

Now it's sold throughout the world in various forms ... from original, low-fat and reduced sodium to turkey-meat versions. SPAM has been the butt of "mystery meat" jokes and Monty Python sketches, as well as a mainstay of most every American mom's breakfast-lunch-dinner repertoire.

In fact, SPAM is such a global icon (you can buy it here in Malaysia, too) the Hormel folks decided it was high time to build a museum to honour it. And they created an annual event, called the SPAM Fest, during which time thousands of the curious (or simply bored) descend upon Austin's farm-friendly community.

George Burns and Gracie Allen were SPAM's commerical U.S. radio spokespersons in the 40's. Today, Hormel - which offers an enormous line of various products - is a sophisticated global marketer.

But are they "sophisticated" enough to use spam to market SPAM?

SPAM, the Ugly.

"spam", as opposed to SPAM (always all uppercase), denotes unwanted commercial email. It's an ugly reality every Internet user has experienced.

We're not talking about website visitors who "opt in" to receive regular or occasional commercial email messages. These people have actually requested the communications they receive. When a marketer "spams" he is emailing to a relatively cold-list of prospects, deemed somehow worth keeping in touch with.

If the same communication was sent via land-mail to the same untargeted list of customers, these marketers would lose their shirts. But because "spamming" is such an inexpensive and uncomplicated process, email marketers figure "what the heck". They may indeed get the "click-thru's" they desire, and actually sell something in the process.

The email marketing industry sends billions of emails. And yes, most of these emails are sent to people who have asked for them.

But times, they are a'changing. In the earlier days of the internet, consumers viewed email promotions very favorably. But as they've been online, they have begun to view emails as having much less relevance.

And what about those consumers who are receiving email promotions they didn't ask for? Complaints have encouraged internet service providers to spend huge amounts on new hardware, software and personnel to fight spam.

Many frustrated consumers vow to never purchase brands that communicate through spam, causing marketers higher acquisition costs to replace them.

But far worse is the marketer's attitude that "spamming" is OK because it's so darn cheap. So what, they say, if the mail is unwanted? It may be difficult to measure the effect of unwanted email on brand perception, but I venture to guess it's a serious problem. Emotions run high when the private world of internet use is invaded by unrequested communications, and the resulting damage to brand names could be irreparable.

If you're the victim of spamming, you're pretty much out of luck. Sure, almost all include an "opt-out" link. But if you click, all you're confirming to many of these marketers is that your address is good. Your email programme may have a spam filter, but these wizards don't always work 100%.

The best solution is at the hands of email marketers. It's time they realized that a good, responsive email list of 10,000 is a helluva lot better - and less damaging to the brand - than a much larger quantity of disinterested consumers. Give the people on your list a real opportunity to opt out and save them and yourself a potential hate-relationship.

And by all means, if you haven't experienced the comparatively innocent joy of SPAM, the Good, give it a try.

How to Raise US$55 Million in 29 Days

T his is not just a true story about an immense amount of cash.

And it's not just about politics, in America or elsewhere. It's about choosing a long-term approach to individuals with whom you wish to have a close - and mutually beneficial - relationship. Whether you are selling candles or candidates.

And while it is a testament to the marketing potential of our increasingly digital world, this story transcends mere media strategy. The case study enlightens the importance of how well we understand the persons we are selling to. How specifically we consider and value knowing who they are, how they feel, what they want.

You be the judge ...

In the 29 days of February 2008, Barack Obama received contributions of more than US$55,000,000 to finance his fight against Hillary Clinton in the U.S. Democratic presidential primaries.

Most of that money - about US$45 million - was raised online. And more than 90 percent of the online donations were for US$100 or less. US$100: a relatively piddling amount from individuals that, together, formed one gigantic money pool.

Traditionally, campaign finance managers have relied on big money sources, large donations from corporations and high net worth individuals. Not this time. 80/20 has been reversed.

The February outpouring of cash shattered Obama's previous recording-breaking January '08 contribution total of US$32 million ... US$28 million of which came from online donors. Again, 90% of these donations were under US$100.

I donated a wee bit to Obama in both Jan and Feb ... also online. But I connected to his campaign in a marketing sense during Sen. John Kerry's failed 2004 attempt to rid the world of a George W. Bush presidency.

A Shared List

I had donated another very small amount to Sen. Kerry's 2004 campaign. After he endorsed Obama for president last year, Kerry apparently shared his online donor database.

The first email I received regarding Obama's campaign was from Senator Kerry, announcing his endorsement of the young Senator from Illinois. The Senator was urging me to support Obama.

More email followed, in a fairly consistent bi- or tri-monthly pattern. From Borack Obama (well, you know, from whomever's really writing them); David Plouffe, his campaign manager; a nameless email from the campaign website "Obama for America"; and even one from Michelle Obama, his wife.

Some emails contain video clips. Obama's speech on race relations was the focus of one. Others are community connected, like a request to help bring out the vote or join a local Obama group.

The Opportunities of
Relationship-Based Online Marketing

According to an article in the online Washington Post, Obama's mix of non-donation emails versus donation emails differed starkly from Clinton's strategy. Her's were, very reliably, an aggressive plea for money.

And while Obama spent more than 10 times as much as Clinton on internet advertising, no one in the history of campaign fundraising has come any where near the donation levels he reached.

Heavy ad spend on cleverly selected web sites, or well-timed, demographically targeted attachments to search terms, no doubt had a major impact on Obama's online donation success. But considering the record-breaking levels of that success, you have to give the campaign credit for resisting the temptation to be all cash-eyed with every email.

Can those of us in a non-political marketing world learn anything from Obama's fundraising campaign?

Yes we can.

BREAKING NEWS:
New Dawgs Learn Old Tricks

So tell me. What arrived in your email in-box today?

What unwanted message from which dubious stranger floated through cyberspace to invade your space? And try to sell you something?

I'll tell you what I get daily. Roughly half express concerns about my erectile disfunction. The other half offers growth solutions for the same organ in question. Up to 3 inches, they proclaim.

Imagine that particular personal double whammy. Forever flaccid and miniscule. Enough to make a grown man (and/or his sexual partner) cry.

These companies are way off target, of course. (No, really.) They send messages like that en masse, regardless of the needs or wants of their recipients. Heck, apparently my sister also has flaccid and miniscule problems because she gets the same sort of email.

But hang on. The real e-commerce pros - the companies who have both Brand and ROI accountability - aren't nearly as carefree about who is emailed what.

Most of the websites and advertising networks on the web will place a cookie on your browser the first time you visit them. The cookie allows them to record your I.P. address and recognize you the next time you arrive. And if you register with a website, they will connect your cookie with your name.

That has been happening since the dawn of cyberspace. Of course, much more is starting to happen now, at least in the U.S.

Louise Story, a technology writer for the New York Times, reports that Web companies are beginning to follow you around as you browse, collecting data on each and every stop you make. The goal of this data collection is to gather individual user interests and actions to offer better targeting opportunities for advertisers. And charge them premium rates.

The downside is, well, someone is watching you. And although the Web companies insist they would never share consumers' names and personal behavior to advertisers, you might be forgiven if you responded to that promise with, "Yeah, right".

Back to commercial emailers. These relatively "new dawgs" in the world of sales and marketing are learning that quite a lot of the "old tricks" of Direct Mail help maximize their success.

The function of a "teaser" printed on a standard Direct Mail envelope has always been to get the darn thing opened. If you can't pique the curiosity of the person you're mailing enough to at least have a look inside, you're dead.

My favorite envelope teaser line of all time was one written by the late (but still god-like) Bill Jayme. His client was a magazine called Psychology Today and the mailing he wrote was for subscription sales. The single line on the envelope was:

Do you close the bathroom door, even when you're the only one home?

Genius. "Why, yes I do!" Or ... "What the ... what's that all about?" Either way, you're going to open that envelope.

What's the email equivalent of a printed envelope? The subject line. Unfortunately, a poetic but powerful teaser like Mr. Jayme's mindbender would simply be too long for a subject line. The point is, major emailers are testing subject lines to hone in on what gets the email opened, then who clicks through or buys something.

The most critical factor that determines the success of Direct Mail is the list you are using. Unlike the marketers of those harder, longer, bigger products, legit emailers are finding ways to target much more precisely. They build lists based on their prospects' opt-in, self-offered preferences, and use predictive software to develop the right message to the right people at the right time. (This has always been Direct Mail's antithetic answer to Junk Mail.)

And the second most important results-booster in Direct Mail is the offer. Commercial email has some distinct advantages here. With Direct Mail, you can split offers to your list and see which works best. But it takes time to get the results. Emailings can also split offers to a portion of your list, get results in a few hours, modify and determine a winner and roll it out to everyone in just a few hours more. Time is money!

Formats can also affect the success of both Direct Mail and email. Full color envelope or just a teaser line? HTML or text only? And the trick with printed letters is "not to dawdle". Get to the point soon. With email: Be sure your most important message is seen before your prospect has to scroll down.

Just goes to prove that whether you're digital or inked, some old truths can still apply. But the way, it is absolutely untrue that you can't teach an old dog new tricks. I'm jumping through new hoops everyday.

Marketers Who Have Money to Burn

I've had nightmares about another economic downturn. Tight money. No confidence. Budgets slashed.

Nevermind all that. Not to worry. Just take a look at some of the advertising that's out there now. Judging by the investments being made for questionably effective communications, there are lots of marketers with money to burn.

I will not name names.

A diaper Brand ran a 5-second-or-so static TV commercial on the Malaysian airwaves a while back. It was just a title shot with a picture of the product, a phone number and a voiceover. I don't know if it ran during business hours, because as much as I'd like to sit around watching daytime television, I'm usually in the office.

The male voice encouraged viewers to call for a free sample. That's the good news. The toll-free number should help identify the Brand's prospects. They can data capture names and addresses, along with baby ages, and mail to them. They could develop a communication programme that would turn prospects into customers and maximize their life-time value. I don't know that the Brand was doing that, but they certainly could, and should have.

The bad news is that the commercial appeared and disappeared in the blink of an eye. If response was the main objective (as it undoubtedly was) the diapers Brand should have demanded that the spot met the minimum response criteria. In this case, it would have to be: Remember the Damn Number to Call.

My mind may not be the steel trap it used to be, but there should be enough grey matter intact to remember a simple phone number. Not on the first viewing, to be sure. "Oh, that's interesting, " I thought to myself. "I'll catch it the next time." Nope. Nor on the third. (They ran it quite frequently in a rather compressed series of slots.)

Pen and paper in hand, ignoring regularly scheduled programming to concentrate on commercial breaks, I was at last successful. The spot came up and went away, as speedily as usual, but I captured it in black and white. Eagerly I grabbed the cordless and began to dial. RingRing. RingRing. RingRing. And some more. No answer. Not even an annoying automated voice response system.

I vowed to try again the next day during office hours. But I forgot my little slip of paper with the phone number on it. And, of course, the number was lost in the dark recesses of my less-than-perfect brain.

I'm not a prospect for baby diapers (or the adult variety for that matter). I have a sign on my office wall that reads: "Unattended Children Will be Sold as Slaves". But I have friends who are. And, had I the opportunity, I would have given up their names and addresses and any other information requested. Their baby is the perfect age for the advertised diaper product, and will remain perfect for months.

What a waste. No one will try as hard as I did to remember or capture that all-important phone number. Chances of remembering would have been greatly improved (and research has proven this) if the number had been included in the voiceover. At least once. Preferably more than once. Even short TVC's can be responsive, but you must use techniques to help viewers remember response information. A flashing number might have helped. Or numbers that appeared one-by-one as the announcer blabbered on.

And Golden Rule Number One: "If You Want Someone to Call You, Make Sure Someone Answers the Call". This is so basic it pains me deeply to see it in print. Most people who respond to toll-free numbers in broadcast media, respond immediately. They do not save the number and call later. They call now. So if you run a responsive spot after normal business hours, make sure your back-end systems are sufficiently sophisticated and properly operated. Otherwise, missed opportunities will vastly outnumber your hits.

And contrary to my cynical opening comments, we all must pay very close attention to our bottom lines these days. But there are right ways, and wrong ways. The right ways don't have to cost a huge amount of money. And the wrong ways are almost always a disappointing and unnecessary waste.

How Your Direct Mail Can Be Like
A Mailing From Mom

I get a lot of junk in my post box. Don't you?

Like flyers from wanna-be English tutors with promises like, "I will learn you English in just 7 sessions."

And the endless little mailings from companies that exist solely to keep my septic tank from overflowing onto the neighbour's bordering bougainvillaea.

Everyone gets junk in the post box. My business partner Mano (who is, by the way, very much a woman) received a good one recently. Addressed to Mr. Mano, the mailing offered an herbal alternative to Viagra. If you could ignore the prefix confusion, I suppose the mailer could almost be forgiven - since the product is "guaranteed" to be effective for women, too. But Ms. Mano was not amused.

All of the above fit our definition of junk mail: The wrong message to the wrong person at the wrong time. But on rare and wonderful occasions, the junk in my post box is joined by spectacular exceptions.

Take, for example, almost every offer sent to me by National Geographic. Being a member and subscriber to their magazine, I also receive opportunities to discover the ancient origins of modern man ... journey step-by-step to the top of the world ... or take a breathtaking tour of the wonders of my own body.

And like their magazine, each and every National Geographic mailing contains stunning photographs and exquisitely written text.

But beyond the obvious creative superiority, what differentiates mailings like the ones I receive from National Geographic from all the junk?

The answers lie hidden in another question, "Do you enjoy getting mail from your mom?"

Of course you do. (Assuming she hasn't gone digital.) With just a quick glance at the envelope, you know who it's from. The postmark and her handwriting, of course, are give-aways.

Being a mailing from mom, the offer is implicit ... "Open this up to hear from someone who has and continues to love and nurture you."

That's answer number one: Familiarity breeds response. You open up mom's mail because you have a "relationship" with her. I'm more likely to respond to a National Geographic mailing for the same reason. Companies that sell to a customer database through a series of well-planned communications enjoy the profits of familiarity.

It also costs less to retain, upgrade and cross-sell to existing customers than it costs to acquire new ones. Existing customers tend to buy more - and more often - than prospects who don't have an established relationship with you.

You know mom, and she knows you, too. (Sometimes too well.) That's answer number two: Don't mail a specific message to just anyone. Be as meticulous and picky as you possibly can about who's on your mailing list.

National Geographic mails to me because I'm a member ... but they also know I've purchased their books. They know how much I've spent with them and when. They know which of their offers have appealed to me in the past.

You can achieve a higher percentage of "hits" - those who say YES to an offer or send you money - by profiling your ideal prospect and segmenting your list towards that profile. You'll also have greater success if you track past results so you can keep doing what works, and stop doing what doesn't.

The third answer is a matter of both content and style. Mom sends you news and information relevant to your "needs and wants". And her style is personal, written from one individual to another - not unlike the National Geographic mailings.

Direct mail letters allow the opportunity to get personal. That's why letters are the single most important element in any mailing. If you don't do letters well, or (horrors!) send a mailing without a letter, you are inviting disaster.

Successful letters refer to you by name, or at least by a relationship or association. They say "you" at least twice more often than "I". They ask you direct questions and request a response. They may tell you a story, make you laugh or cry, involve you in a solution, explain a tricky problem - but above all, inspire you to act and act now.

Back to Basics:
The Anatomy of a Letter

It's time to get back to some fundamentals. This retro intention is inspired by a direct mail pack I recently received from a "major telecommunications company".

The mail pack was innocuous enough, with the usual elements: outer envelope, brochure, registration form and letter. Unfortunately, being innocuous is no substitute for "sell", and absolutely intolerable if Harmless = Boring.

And the letter. The most important element of any direct mail pack. To begin with, they personalised my name in the salutation, but included my middle name. Hardly any real person I know refers to me as "Dear Kurt Douglas Crocker" - with or without the proper comma ending they omitted.

My gawd, I'm ranting again. I guess I just can't help myself. The entire tone of this letter was studiously passive. It read as if the writer was half asleep, droning the recipient (in this case, me) into his state of semi-consciousness. The beginning of a letter, for example, should evoke the silent response, "Oh, that sounds interesting" rather than "It's time for my nap."

It would have helped the writer to know that, while letters are not advertisements, they can be structured using that time-honoured "great ads" formula: Attention, Interest, Desire, Conviction, Action.

The all-important first paragraph should command "Attention". According to the co-editor of "Million Dollar Mailings", most letters in the U.S. grab attention by appealing to flattery, or greed, or both. This can be accomplished by a number of techniques. By stating some important news, or a startling statistic, or humour (tricky, but it can work) or by telling a story (even trickier).

But whatever technique is used, the beginning of a letter must get to the point quickly, in a very interesting manner. A easy tip: Half your problem will be solved if you use short words, short sentences and short paragraphs.

The afore-mentioned offending letter began with a sentence that contained a mind-numbing 33 words. But enough of the wrong way. Let's examine a letter that does it right. It's one of my all-time favourites, written a very long time ago for The American Film Institute (AFI membership/magazine subscription) by (ostensibly) Francis Ford Coppola.

Unfortunately, I can't share the entire letter. It's four pages long. And don't give me that crap about "no one reads long copy". If you're talking to the right person - in this case, film lovers - in the right way, you can sell from salutation to signature no matter how long the damn thing is.

AFI's letter begins with a classic "Johnson Box", a headline area of copy that's usually above the salutation. And, my what a surprise, it appeals to flattery:

You are one of a select group
recently nominated for National Membership
in the American Film Institute.

Then, the beginning:

Dear Mr. Crocker,

A darkened room, a parting curtain. Even now - after years in the profession, after directing The Godfather and Apocalypse Now - the opening moments of a movie never fail to cast their spell on me.

That's why I'm delighted to invite you to join a group of people who want to be closer to, and better enjoy, an art form that touches all our lives.

Is that great, or what? A short story, with a compelling image. Then a second paragraph that gets directly to business and benefits.

The next few paragraphs are "transition to detail", where Attention shifts to Interest and Desire:

Your new membership in The American Film Institute will put you in this picture....an insider to the exciting arts and dynamic industries of film, TV and video.

> *On behalf of AFI's Board of Trustees,*
> *I need to hear in the next ten days*
> *if you will accept their special nomination.*

But first, let me tell you about some of the many member benefits they've already reserved for you:

Then the details begin. Invitations to film screenings, generous discounts, reduced-price admission to AFI Theaters, and of course, a subscription to American Film Magazine.

Page two and three are devoted to Desire and Conviction, with more details about the magazine and AFI's film preservation activities. The urgency of saving rare movie prints is written about in stunning form:

With your support, we can save the magic moments of Gene Kelly's Singing in the Rain, and Fred Astaire dancing in Swing Time. Bogey coming face to face with Bergman, Judy Garland on the road to Oz, even Lucy and Ethel stuffing chocolates in their uniforms as the conveyor belt speeds by.

And page four is all action. Quick reminders of key benefits. A review of the cost of membership, and all that it includes. A note that membership is offered at an exclusive rate. My only quibble: No re-mention of the sender's request to respond within 10 days, though I suspect that's because they'll solicit again if there is no response.

From start to finish, this is one helluva letter, and could easily represent a benchmark for any letter written for the purpose of sales.

And some food for thought. There's a lot of crap delivered in the mail, truly "junk" by anyone's standards. But the same can easily be said about e-commerce mail, including the stuff that's sent by request from a website. Wouldn't it be wise to remember the basics, and send more email that follows the form of a great sales letter?

Is Our World Losing Its Lunacy?

Some would argue that you'd have to be nuts to be in advertising. And that you'd have to be absolutely raving to have anything to do with Direct Marketing.

Believe me, crazy helps.

Some of the earliest words uttered about Direct Marketing came from David Ogilvy. He said, "I'm passionate about Direct. It was my first love and secret weapon."

What a nut case. He mailed homing pigeons to big company CEO's to sell airplanes. But Direct Marketing helped propel his agency to heady heights. And this wonderfully delirious man held the creative reins while it happened.

Jerry Della Femina, though never a Direct Marketer, had a bit of the old legume in him as well. He wrote a book about advertising wars a long time ago. It was called *From Those Wonderful Folks Who Gave You Pearl Harbor*.

There's a notorious story about Della Femina. As it goes, he happened to stroll into a room at his N.Y. agency and surprised two of his staff members who were having sex on the photocopy machine.

Their coitus interrupted, the two lovebirds feared the worst. Instead, Jerry just smiled and said, "It does my heart good to see two of my employees so at ease and comfortable here, they dare to enjoy a moment like this in my agency." (Or words to that effect.)

Crazy, huh? But Jerry Della Femina produced some very historically creative advertising back in the 70's and 80's.

Yazmin and Ali, the two powerful and (I would imagine) decadently rich creative gurus at award-winning Leo Burnett Malaysia, were an odd pairing that gave birth to brilliant results. He, a quiet, reflective, friendly but introspective fella. She, an out-going, singer-musician, rapier wit. Diametrically opposed personalities who have created some of Malaysia's best work. Simply insane.

And then there's Bill Jayme (pronounced "Jamie") and Heikki (rhymes with "flaky") Ratalahti. Another crazy pair. But a pair who have been called "the copywriter and art director who changed direct mail forever" ... and "the creative team of the century".

These guys, alas, no longer with us, dared to ignore the rules. Jayme tossed out the sale-pitch approach to letters and instead wrote captivating narratives. And the envelope teasers! Here's a sampling:

* In giant type on an envelope for McGraw-Hill's Business Week, just one word: DAMN! This was followed up in the letter. The copy began: "Do you find a perfect stock you are tempted to buy ... and you put it off for a day or two ... and it goes up ... and find yourself saying, 'DAMN!' Well, now's the time to stop saying damn ..."

- The famous outer envelope teaser for Psychology Today: "Do you close the bathroom door even when you're the only one home?"

- An envelope teaser for Earthwatch, one of the longest ever:

Got some free time?
A week? A month? A summer?
Come volunteer for a
conservation project in the wilds.
An environmental study in the tropics.
An archaeological dig abroad.
Or, if you're busy now,
cheer us on from the sidelines.

Jayme's and Heikki's clients were standing in line for a single direct mail package.

So what's the point? In each example of creative genius I've mentioned, either the individual or the team was delightfully off-centre. And in each case, this lunatic edge is the direct result of a deeply rooted love for the work ... a characteristic that seems increasingly rare here in Malaysia.

Intense passion for what we do is the only way to produce intensely brilliant work. Evidence of such passion is hard enough to notice in the world of advertising. In Direct Marketing, well, there are so few of us around, it's hard to get the numbers for a reliable sample. But there's certainly not a lot of true-love for the craft.

If there were a lot of love emanating from DM creative teams here, the work wouldn't be so bloody boring. In a rare interview with Target Marketing magazine (October 2000 issue), Bill Jayme put it this way:

"I'll tell you what really irks me. Few copywriters today seem to care.
How many times have I heard a colleague say to me, 'I'd love to have
another drink with you, but I have to knock out a package tonight.'
My god, Heikki and I spent two weeks getting it right. I cared about
every single word. Heikki knew every single line and every typeface."

And this is from the crazy man who had a dazzling home on 5 acres of land in the heart of Sonoma Valley. Get the point?

If 95% Of All Advertising Is Crap, What About Direct Marketing?

A couple of years ago, Mark Waites, creative director at Mother London and a MC2 * judge, was quoted in an online article at Boardsmag.com.

"Advertising is like every other creative endeavor: 95% of the results are shit," he reportedly lamented. "You get blamed for everybody else's bad work, which is ironic, because I don't think Michael Stipe gets blamed for the Backstreet Boys.

For the musically challenged amongst you, Michael Stipe is the iconic and enormously talented lead singer/songwriter of the still-going-strong rock group R.E.M. And the Backstreet Boys are, well, the Backstreet Boys.

I cannot respond with "Yeah, I know the feeling", because I'm not even close to a realm where I would assume myself the Michael Stipe of the Direct Marketing world. And yet, just a few days ago, my brother, the ever-testy Patrick Teoh**, laid the 95% crap label on Direct Marketing in Malaysia, and called on me to account for it.

First of all, I could not disagree. Just as no one who loves great advertising could disagree with Mark Waites. All you have to do is open your eyes to see the vastness of bad work being done under the banners of Advertising and Direct Marketing - DM being simply another form of Advertising.

Mark may be currently blameless for bad advertising (he does assume, though doesn't quite remember, that his first ad was "embarrassing for sure"). But there I was, face-to-face with Mr. T, being held responsible for the worst of this country's mind-boggling Direct Marketing badness.

Maybe you do get blamed for everybody else's bad work. I couldn't help thinking, though, that my contemplated "voice in the wilderness" defense shouldn't fly. The dynamics required for brilliant creative work - responsive or not - are still graspable in Malaysia, despite real or imagined roadblocks.

So let me stay on a positive track as I attempt, again, to identify and topple down some of those roadblocks ...

Timidity

I have heard, many times over the years, that bold, outrageous, and therefore frequently awesome advertising is impossible in Malaysia. Clients won't buy it. Agency teams - including creative - won't sell it. And it's too often culturally unacceptable. It is time to stop being scared about who'll think what and just do it.

Arrogance

Too many people who know too little don't listen to those who know much more. In some cases, the small-minded in positions of power actually believe they have the capacity to reach the right conclusions. In most cases, it's a positioning tactic, intended to solidify their proximity to the pole.

If you want to leap ahead of these annoying blockheads, make the effort to play their silly games. But always keep your eye on the finish line.

Greed

Quick money is the reason why so many brand leaders are currently engaged in promotional pissing contests with their competitors. There is nothing wrong with a promotion. But you cannot conduct a free toaster war without a vividly clear idea about where you are taking your brand, long-term. Never lose sight of your brand's future, even when you're being tactical.

Sloth

Where have all the lean and hungry gone? There has been a stark and frightening change of attitude through all levels within agency and client organizations. It seems that many believe that "looking busy" is the best guarantee of a salary increment and upgraded job title.

And yes, all this "motional" effort ends up producing results that are "95% crap". More emotion. Less motion. Please, find the passion once again, and employers: reward accordingly.

Underexposure

You've probably heard the old advertising chestnut: "Search the world and steal the best." Well, don't do that. But more of you who create advertising should make a concerted study of work that has been judged stunningly effective. Be inspired by the courage of it, imagine the thrill of the creative process involved, ponder the richness and rewards enjoyed by everyone who said, "Yes!".

Then come up with your own ideas that make theirs look pale by comparison.

Author's Note:

*   *MC2 or Malaysian Creative Circle Awards was organized by ADOI magazine to reward creative excellence. After a few years, it was discontinued.*

**   *Patrick Teoh, my close, personal friend, was once the top national DJ and known as "The Voice of Malaysia". He's still widely revered as a local/regional theater, TV and movie actor, who has (to date) also appeared in a couple of Hollywood films ... Return to Paradise and Anna and the King. I am the proud godfather of Mr. T's son Adam.*

My Secret Love Affair with "Yours Sincerely"

I confess. All forms of creation give me cause for emotional stirrings. But only one really makes my heart go "boom".

Some love television commercial creation. Well, so do I, especially the long ones ... 60 seconds minimum, even better at 120. The kind that wraps itself around the viewer's needs and wants and commands an action only the unduly cynical - or declared dead - could possibly ignore.

Some love page space. I do, too, especially the creation of print advertising that causes an irresistible urge to cut, fax, call or visit a website.

Self-gratification can be fun ... but be warned

Radio can also be self-gratifying, a writer's opportunity to create on his or her own - without the benefit of an art director partner. Doing radio ads can be a lot of fun, perhaps too much fun. If fact, many radio ad writers have so much fun they forget about what they're selling.

But there's another partner-less form of creation that demands a writer's complete concentration. It's the one that begins, more often than not, with "dear" and ends with "yours sincerely".

Letters. What's not to love about letters?

Letters are also a writer's playground. But they are far less susceptible to frivolous creation because the sole purpose of a letter is to close the sale.

As with any love affair, you can only truly appreciate the beauty of letters if you spend some serious time writing them. And you will only be completely fulfilled if you master one of the most difficult stages of the affair ... the beginning.

Satisfaction begins at the beginning

There are many satisfying ways to begin a letter. Alex Anderson, co-editor of "Million Dollar Mailings" claimed that nearly all the most successful letters in the U.S. open with either flattery, an appeal to greed or both.

Strong letters open with a benefit, or at least a strongly implied benefit. You could open with "news." One of the most difficult ways to begin a letter is to "tell a story" ... a story that both intrigues and directly engages the reader.

Only the very best writers should attempt to begin a letter using a story technique. Your tale must command attention, and at the same time, should start to build towards a logical argument that will help close the sale. If you've attempted a story beginning, read it out loud to a colleague who will tell you the truth about what you've written. Then question any positive comments and rewrite. You can always do better.

Tell me a story

One of the true gurus of letters that begin with a story was also one of the richest. He and his partner charged up to US$40,000 per direct mail package (for just copy writing and art direction) ... and that was years ago. I'm convinced his letter writing skills were no small justification for the cost.

But don't take my word for it. Read these beginnings by the acclaimed copywriter Bill Jayme and judge for yourself. All are for magazine subscriptions. Keep in mind that he wrote these stories for a very targeted someone, whose interests (by list selection) are suspected.

Bon Appetit
(Recipes and articles about food and drink)

First, fill a pitcher with ice.
Now pour in a bottle of ordinary red wine, a quarter cup of brandy and a small bottle of club soda.
Sweeten to taste with a quarter to a half cup of sugar, garnish with slices of apple, lemon, orange ... then move your chair to a warm, sunny spot.
You've just made yourself a Sangria - one of the great glories of Spain, and the perfect thing to sit back with and sip while you consider this invitation.

Worth
(Money-related features and articles)

It was Scott Fitzgerald who observed, "The rich are different from us."
It was Earnest Hemingway who then shot back, "Yes they have more money."
But money isn't all that the rich have more of. They also have more worries ...
So before you accept this invitation to move up higher financially, you may want to consider some of the pros and cons.

Andy Warhol's Interview
(Interviews with the artsy-fartsy, in-crowd)

When you find yourself seated at dinner next to someone unusual like Bette Midler, you've got two choices.

You can ask what her brother Danny is up to, why she worships Bobby Darin, whether they really paid for her in gold for her recent round-the-world tour, why she thinks Paloma Picasso should design clothes, where her favorite hot dog stand is in LA, and how she feels about Barbra Streisand.

Or ... you can say, "Excuse me. Can you please pass the salt?"

A Rubik Offer You Can't Refuse

Quite a few years ago I gave my now-departed brother-in-law a Rubik's cube for Christmas. I really loved my brother-in-law but I gave it to him anyway.

Rubik's cube was invented by a sadistic and probably mad scientist. The guy subsequently made millions of dollars when he sold it as a puzzle to equally sadistic gift-givers like me.

The object is to twist and turn the thing until each side of the cube becomes a single colour. My poor brother-in-law struggled with it for five days straight until he finally managed the task.

ASTRO (Malaysia's satellite television programming provider) once used a Rubik cube-like graphic to symbolize the mix-and-match qualities of their latest "flexi package" offer. Considering the nature and intent of their offer, I'd say the symbolism is spot on.

Subscribers received a direct mail package announcing this "whole new way to enjoy ASTRO". The Rubik cube-like graphic emblazons the front of a window envelope and a teaser instructs you to "Open now to mix and match".

The cube graphic has images popping out of it and it's already begun to turn. In other words, your mind has already begun to boggle.

Two of the elements inside are nicely personalized - the letter and a response form. The letter begins with a 4-line name and address that appears through the outer envelope, and salutes the receiver's name personally. The Rubik's graphic is there again, and the first puzzle turns up in the lead sentence.

The letter begins:

Dear Mr. Kurt Crocker,

Over the years you have given us a lot of feedback on how you wish to enjoy your ASTRO service even more.

Well it just ain't so. I've never given ASTRO any feedback at all, directly. Unless there's some electronic device in the decoder that can detect my occasional grumblings about programmes I'd like to see aired - or a least not interrupted in mid-season. I suppose their use of "you" was a universal "you", but it seemed rather odd coming right after my imprinted name.

But that's not the half of it. The truly Rubik puzzlement appears in both the letter and response form, and is the essence of their offer.

What ASTRO was doing is what we direct marketers call a "negative option". This used to be a common tactic for mail-order book clubs. Members of these clubs would subscribe for a promised "book-of-the-month" which would be automatically mailed unless they did not respond. It was a clever tactic indeed, which relied on the very natural human tendency for inaction.

But the difference between what the book clubs used to do and what ASTRO was doing with their flexi package promotion is vastly different. Unless I missed something in the fine print of my original subscription agreement, I never agreed to automatic delivery of a new - and in this case more expensive - service.

What I did agree to do originally was to try out ASTRO and my choice of packages for a period of a few months. For free. My understanding then was that what I signed for would automatically become payable every month after the trial period. But I agreed to that up-front.

Then ASTRO planned to convert me to their recommended package unless I chose a different package altogether.

But there's more to ponder.

Let's take a look at the response form. What they chose on my behalf was:

1) "Movie package & Dynasty package with any 3 mini packages" or
2) "Movie package with all 5 mini packages".

What I receive now is the Movie package & Dynasty package with all 5 mini packages. Hmmmmm. So either I accepted their recommendation of "Dynasty, Movie, 5 Mini Packages" or I miss out on Dynasty or two of the mini packages. That would have to be my choice if I wanted to continue paying RM89.95 per month as opposed to RM99.95 per month for their "new and recommended" packages.

It must be noted that whatever "choice" I made - do nothing or mix 'n match - I would receive a few new "ASTRO Favourite" channels included "free": Discovery Travel and Adventure, tech TV and AXN. And the Dynasty package also includes a couple of new channels: Xing He and TVB8.

In other words, if I do nothing and accept their recommendation I will get Discovery Travel and Adventure, tech TV and AXN "free" plus Xing He and TVB8 - for RM10 more per month.

But wouldn't it have been simpler - and more straightforward - for ASTRO to tell me what they are adding to my current subscription and announce an increased rate? And wouldn't it have been nicer to offer me the option to say "no thanks, I like things as they are" - if ASTRO could do that without technical complications?

Don't get me wrong. I love my ASTRO. And now I'll have a chance to enjoy CSI on AXN ... assuming it lasts a full season.

Author's Note:

* *ASTRO eventually revised their stategy and offered customers pre-change choice of programming.*

** *The complete and latest seasons of all three CSI's are currently running on ASTRO.*

How to Write to Sell

T here are many others more qualified than I to go on about writing. That is, there are many others more qualified to explain the ins and outs of someone responsible for the words required to actually sell something.

But since this book has my name on it, I'll be presumptuous and take up the burden.

This is the thing. Any advice about how to write to sell applies equally to you MASS writers as it does to writers who TARGET prospects and nurture customer RELATIONSHIPS.

This is assuming, of course, that writers who create communications for the masses have in their minds an intention to actually sell something. Which, more often than not, is vividly not the case. Increasingly, advertisements here in Malaysia, and around the world, are written for either 1) A client's approval or 2) Another attempt to win some global reward.

So here is the first tip for writers who want to be a great big ballsy success in the business of advertising:

**Get it into your head that your
primary job is to actually SELL something**

In theory, no one has more knowledge or insight about a Client's products or services than the Client. But that's just theory. Great writers are the most inquisitive people on earth.

**Gain more knowledge about your client's
Products or Services than they proclaim to have**

You are a hack if you don't know what you're writing about. Knowledge is power. Knowledge drives great writing. Do meticulous research. Demand it of your Client. And if your Client doesn't have the knowledge you require, do your research. Ask your Client Services person to help. If he or she doesn't see the need, make a plan to get he or she fired.

**Hone your ability to
make powerful arguments**

Pick a topic. Any topic. Choose a topic to which everyone can make a case against. Argue in your mind or in writing the case for eating chocolate donuts with colorful sprinkles. Defend the policies and personality of George W. Bush. (Try it! Even I, a Bush-a-Phobe can do it.) Choose the cause or product or service you most dislike and defend it.

But do not lie. Do not obscure the facts. Do not even attempt to bend the truth. Deal with the reality of what it is you are selling. I will give you an example. I will write about George W. Bush, a man I personally feel has done incredible harm to my country. Read this as a way to describe his legacy, perhaps published after his term as President has ended:

George W. Bush is a man who desired a lofty goal: To introduce all nations of the world to the limitless personal powers that come with a democratic nation. Every effort he made throughout his presidency was intent on making our international community free of aggression and discontent. He will be judged by history.

Aack! I'm
Gagging now!

To think I would be defending George W. Bush! Aargh! If you will read again, I did not lie. The impact of Bush's policies I alluded to in that blurb was left to historians. Personally, I believe he will be judged the worst U.S. President ever.

But this is the point. Don't. If you feel you cannot write about something you really don't believe in. Don't. But this is also the point. If you are encountered with a product or service that is weak, could be improved upon, not devilish (aka Bush), you must find the positive aspects of it. And sell it.

So. Being a writer who sells is being a person able to develop a convincing argument. And a person dependent on knowledge and a commitment to find whatever truth there is to find. Truth plus full knowledge of bad truths. And in the end, honesty must rule.

The Power of Words

Finally, once you have a grasp on whatever reality you are dealing with, you must have the ability to put words together. But I will tell you this. If you have the "argument" laid out in your head, the words will more easily follow.

I will give you the usual basics. When the words come into your head, keep them active, rather than passive. Give rather than giving. Save rather than savings. Be intense on nouns and verbs, and be very judicious about adjectives. Make descriptive words sharp and relevant.

Don't waste your reader's time. Get to the point. But be conversational. Friendly. Imagine to whom you are talking (writing). Imagine he/she is your aunt/uncle, sister/brother, mom/dad, best friend/lover.

And most of all, remember you are selling something.

Secrets: How to Cry on Cue

I once publically dissed satellite TV broadcasting. The COO of ASTRO, Malaysia's very own satellite broadcaster, wrote to me, lovingly, promising an unassailable explanation of the merits of "DTH over cable". He added that he was "intrigued as to the link between rain fade and Direct Marketing".

The article in question had me fuming about disruptions to my regularly scheduled viewings of, I don't know, "Friends". Or whatever. Interrupted by storms. "Rain fade". I artfully segued into some jabbering about my marketing speciality.

So here's another disconnected coupling: the art of crying on cue, and its relationship to Direct Marketing (or advertising, for that matter).

This is the thing. Just to keep my stress level at its absolute maximum, I occasionally take to the professional stage. I act (or make that attempt). In one role, I had to cry on cue, every night plus two matinees, for 15 days in a row.

I used no specific technique for achieving those tears. But then I thought back about how they came to flow. My strange and scary mind drew a parallel to what we do, or should do, to create compelling communications.

1. Do your research. Know as much as you can about the person you are trying to convince. And I do mean person, singular. Don't ever make the mistake of talking to the masses. Gather all the facts you can about your most likely prospect and create a mental picture of his or her past, present and future.

   On stage, I was The Duke of Norfolk in A Man For All Seasons, trying to convince my closest friend, Sir Thomas Moore to "give in" for friendship's sake ... and to avoid the risk of execution.

2. Empathize. Once you've identified the hard facts, imagine that person's needs and wants. Connect with your prospect's hopes and dreams, and link them to your own. Form an emotional bond with the person to whom you are talking. Find common ground. If your prospect's needs and wants are nothing near your own, ask yourself, "But what if they were?" Look him in the eye; get into his mind.

   Sir Thomas Moore was risking the wrath of King Henry VIII by remaining silent about his monarch's divorce. Torn between loyalty to his King and his faith, with Norfolk caught in-between, Moore denounced his friend with the hope of saving him.

3. Say it with feeling. Express yourself, in words and pictures, with the emotional tone that will convince your prospect to do what you want him to do. State your case logically, countering every possible objection in an orderly way, but say it with a sense of joy or excitement or fear or sadness. Make sure the tone you use is appropriate, but give your message a "voice".

The Duke continued to love and respect Sir Thomas, but their friendship was severed. (Eventually, Moore's head was severed as well.)

Again, these three "secrets" apply to both Direct Marketers and you general practitioners. So give them a serious try and see how they sell. Maybe you'll cry less often.

The crying scene from "A Man For All Seasons"

Photo: Courtesy of Phin

The DM Copywriter: Myths & Realities

W hen's the last time you had an intimate chat with a Direct Marketing Copywriter?

Have you ever met one?

I'm talking about a person whose singular task is to write copy designed to solicit an immediate response. One who gets his or her kicks by actually selling something now, or by motivating someone to get information. I said now. By print or broadcast or digital word. A person who absolutely goes orgasmic at the thought of inducing customers to keep coming back for more and more ... and more.

Can you remember a name? If you can, please give it to me. I am currently chronicling rare and unusual specimens in Malaysia, of the DM copywriter kind. My findings indicate a need for filing an application with the World Health Organisation to include the aforementioned critter on their Endangered Species list. Before which, I must try to document their existence in this country.

I have a lot of work ahead of me.

Having said that (god I hate that terribly British prelude to explanations) I would like to clarify the specific characteristics to look for as you search for that elusive DM copywriter creature. Or imagine yourself as one of them. Here in Malaysia. Because, as it is with all rarely experienced lifeforms, there are many imagined myths attached to them. As one of the few living representatives here of this very lonely community, I hereby offer you a few contradictory realities.

Myth: DM Copywriters are Nerds
Reality: Am not!

Ah, go tell it to your therapist. So what if everyone thinks you're odd just because your nipples twitch when someone buys something because you wrote about it. Things could be worse. You could write about something that no one buys and win big international ad awards. Now how embarrassing would that be?

Truth is, and I humbly offer myself as Exhibit A, DM Copywriters are notoriously cool. We simply exude sex and charisma. When we walk, when we talk, when we're on the dance floor, we are clearly at the centre of all worlds. Until we fall down a carelessly constructed stairway or over our own wildly knotted neckties.

Myth: DM Copywriters are Vampires
Reality: Wanna Neck?

It's a sweet taste, blood is. And Buffy just slays me. But blame this myth on the man himself, Mr. O. He's the one who proclaimed (and I paraphrase cuz I'm too damned lazy to look up the quote), "Everyone who writes advertising copy should cut his teeth in Direct Marketing. They know how to sell. They've tasted blood."

Unfortunately, I must take exception to the great one, on two counts. First, his very apt advice has cast a dubious shadow over the lot of us who claim to be DM copywriters. Second, let's say, just for argument sake, that he was right. Let's say we do have an insatiable desire for the taste of blood, that remarkable feeling of a measured response to our written messages.

Why would anyone cut his teeth, then move on to the relatively lifeless world of advertising? Oh they do, I know. But they then become virtual vampires, and are soon overpowered by the simplicities of mere image and awareness. I'm sure their experience in our netherworld will help them to a degree, if only they remember that taste of corpuscles.

Myth: DM Copywriters Don't Know When to Shut Up
Reality: I take particular exception to this myth as it is an obvious attempt to malign and impeach an otherwise noble vocation which not only benefits marketers and the sons and daughters of marketers and their grandchildren and great-grandchildren but also improves society as a whole, which does indeed, if truth be told, need quite a bit of help.

We do too know when to shut up. So there. This slap-me-on-the-face-and-call-me-wordy insult probably originates from the DM copywriter's proclivity to produce long-copy press ads. Or long-copy letters. Or longer-than-average TV ads. Those overrated non-responsive ad writers get away with a paragraph or two.

All great writers choose short words. Short sentences. Short paragraphs. (Hey, I was just kidding with the above crosshead, OK?) And I mean great copywriters, even of the DM variety. However, if you want someone to actually do something, now, you usually must offer a convincing argument. The tougher the sell, the longer the copy.

But it's not true that we don't know when to shut up. We do. So I will.

We Are a Sad Lot.
Let's Do Something About It

I've worked with all kinds of people.

When I first started, I worked with fellow writers who were as excited about creating greatness as they were about winning at Scrabble. (There were tournaments nearly every lunch hour.)

We seemed to move together, in our enthusiasm, in our kindred desire to out do each other in the friendliest of ways.

Great loves thrived. We were in competition, there is no doubt in that, but we reveled. We reveled about our shared strengths. We celebrated freedom, when it came to us, after hours, days, of dedication to our craft.

When I first came to Malaysia, there was still that sense of adventure and fun. I remember my first drive-by introduction to this country by my Art Director, Choong, and his protégé, Kien. "Look! Merdeka Square. Our Fourth of July! Also, many boy girls."

I understood instantly.

We went on to win the first ever international award for a Malaysian advertising agency in Direct Marketing. The 1st Prize in the global Caples Awards. And top metal Echos.

Landmarks. But it was that remarkable combination of desire, determination and friendship that made that happen.

It wasn't all success, mind you. But when success happened, joy ensued.

The Country Head of the Ogilvy & Mather office at the time wished to reward us and contribute to our celebration with a prize. He insisted that our company paid trip to Penang remain a secret. But it was offered and we accepted, joyfully.

For the record, damning secrets for good sense, that man was Tony Hemmings. Smart fellow. Knows the value of a smile increased.

So there we went. We drove what was, then, the cursed and dangerous road to Penang. And we partied. It was during that weekend, in my humble opinion, and mind you, this was around 1989, that I innocently introduced Tequila to my unsuspecting Malaysian colleagues.

Lick between your thumb and the next finger. Sprinkle salt on the area licked. Grasp a lime wedge on the same hand. Take the shot of Tequila with your free hand. Lick the salt. Drink the shot. Squeeze the lime.

Don't get the wrong idea. It wasn't the partying - or the Tequila - that brought us together. It was our mutual love, for the work, and yes, for each other. Maybe not a hug-hug kind of love, but a love that nurtured us, empowered us, fueled by a common desire, to create and have fun doing it.

Choong ended up doing the most unlikely thing. Some several months later, he died. Complications from Chicken Pox. I remember when he called me to say he wouldn't be coming in for a few days. Chicken Pox. I said, well, rest. Don't itch. And we'll see you when you get back.

Then suddenly he was in intensive care. I was told, just a precaution. Then the phone call. The memories of that phone call still invade me. I go about my business on most days, but sometimes that phone call just floods my brain. So young. So talented. So interested. So intent. So curious. So much desire. Gone.

Life, and death, is so pitifully unpredictable. Here and now is a vital grounding.

And now, I find myself associated, on a number of occasions, with an onslaught of individuals who are in a position of either creating or approving ideas. My judgment of these individuals is always based on two clear and simple questions: 1) Are they driven by great, unselfish intentions? And 2) Do they take this seriously, but with a sense of humor?

Sadly, and I'm talking about both clients and agency folk, I seldom see drives that are in any way directed toward greatness, and are almost always selfish. But most upsetting of all is that there seems to be no humor available from anyone. We can do serious work, and produce serious results, and still have fun, can't we?

We are people. Individuals. We have our jobs to do. We must be dedicated to producing sales and expect our due rewards. But our jobs should be done with smiles, all around. And the smiles seem to have diminished at best; vanished at worst.

Well, I, for one, intend to protract what has become a smirk, into a smile again. I hope you all do the same. Have fun. Here and now. If not again, for the first time.

Kurt, the "sandwiched" name in the advertising and direct marketing firm Drayton Bird, Crocker & Mano Sdn. Bhd. (DBC&M), has been working and playing in Malaysia since 1989.

Kurt Crocker founded DBC&M with Drayton Bird, an internationally renowned best-selling author and direct marketing guru, and Mano Stickney in 1995.

Kurt helms DBC&M in Kuala Lumpur with Mano, blending his 30-plus years of direct marketing experience into the agency's award-winning creative work.

Prior to DBC&M, Kurt was Executive Director and Executive Creative Director for what was then dubbed Ogilvy & Mather Direct, Kuala Lumpur (now OgilvyOne). He joined them after discovering the tropical pleasures of Malaysia during his 2-year stint in Hong Kong as a regional creative resource for O&M Direct.

Kurt began his decade-long tenure with O&M in their L.A. office. He had been transported there from his home-state of Minnesota, where he was a copywriter and direct marketing specialist for Colle & McVoy Advertising in Minneapolis. Direct marketing experience ahead of that includes ABC Publishing (a former division of the U.S. national television network) and Fingerhut, one of the largest direct mail companies in the world.

In addition to being a regular speaker, lecturer and long-time direct marketing columnist for a Malaysian trade publication called ADOI magazine, Kurt has also been known to strut his stuff on Malaysian stage and small screen.

"Direct Marketing in Malaysia (And Other Amazing Stories)" is Kurt's first book.

Cover Design: Melvin Liew